Unconven

CW01095261

By

Mark Williams BCAH FRSA

A Memoir of Post-Traumatic Growth, ADHD, and Resilience

Dedicated to all the people who believed in me, and to those who didn't who made me stronger.

un·con·ven·tion·al

not based on or conforming to what is generally done or believed:

"His unconventional approach to life"

ADJECTIVE

If you describe a person or their attitude or behaviour as unconventional, you mean that they do not behave in the same way as most other people in their society.

ADJECTIVE

An unconventional way of doing something is not the usual way of doing it and may be rather surprising.

The Author

Mark Williams BCAh FRSA is a Keynote Speaker, Author and International campaigner.

Born in early seventies, struggled in school, and left at fifteen years of age, in the same year he became a British champion. It was only at the age of forty years of age, he was diagnosed with ADHD and Dyslexia.

After working in a factory for six years, started his successful sales career and has worked in youth and mental health services since 2005. He has a livid experience of anxiety and depression, while learning from academics and most importantly the people he has supported over the years.

In 2010, he became very unwell and entered community mental health services. He founded International Fathers Mental Health Day and #Howareyoudad campaign to make sure all parents are having support for the whole family.

Mark has spoken on television and radio stations around the world while working with Dr Jane Hanley who have both published articles on Fathers Mental Health together. Mark was awarded Inspirational Father of the year and local hero at the Pride of Britain Awards in 2012 even invited to meet The Royal Family on World Mental Health Day also awarded the Point Of light Award by the Prime Minister in 2019.

Mark published the report called "Fathers Reaching Out - Why Dads Matter" to explain the importance of paternal mental health which far better outcomes for the whole family and the development of the child has when we include fathers.

Mark has contributed to over twenty books about fathers' mental health. He has trained, Midwives and Health Visitors on paternal mental health and other professionals. Also, as a consultant for many organisations including the National Health Service, Movember, Tommy Tippe while delivering talks to companies including Google.

Helped produce the film Daddy Blues based on Mark journey is now available on Amazon Prime. Ambassador for Mother's for Mother's and Mother Matter charities. Started the Campaign to reopen the mother and baby unit in Wales, which was reopened seven years later.

Mark has recently spoken at the largest European ADHD conference alongside Dr Tony Lloyd and Dr Ned Hallowell. He has written articles on the subject and is a research champion on ADHD at the University of Cardiff.

In 2023, Mark was awarded the British Citizens Award for Healthcare at Westminster for work in changing policies and becoming a pioneer in mental health. He is now a member of the Fatherhood All Party Parliamentary Group and a Human Rights activist.

Mark is happily married with Michelle, who also works in youth and mental health services. They have one son, Ethan who they love so much and enjoys sport, music and socializing while working full time with his business. Mark may not be richest financially, but far richer in life. He also cleans his youth club with his wife Michelle fortnightly.

He is now also a development speaker and consultant for businesses around mental health, neurodiversity and growth. His aims are to have the freedom to do the things that he enjoys, while helping other grow.

"When one door closes, another opens; but we often look so long and so regretfully upon the closed door that we do not see the one which has opened for us." – Alexander Graham Bell

Foreword

Mark Williams's enthusiasm and passion is more than enough to fuel a PowerStation to supply energy to the whole world. Since I have known Mark, his desire to make a difference has been unwavering.

I was introduced to him as we both had a special interest in fathers' mental health. At that time, little was known about this as a 'condition', as most of the research and support focused on mothers' mental health. The recognition of the mental health of mothers during the perinatal period was in its infancy, with reputable researchers and clinicians highlighting the importance of good mental health in both pregnancy and during the postnatal period.

Some of the consequences of mental illnesses and disorders for mothers and infants were accepted, and health care professionals and practitioners were able to adapt their practice to accommodate the needs of the mothers and their infants. The role of fathers was not, on the whole acknowledged.

There was little regard for their mental health and how that may be affected by the process of the pregnancy, delivery and postnatal period. When perinatal mental health support services were in place, there were few for fathers. Fathers were often not included in the conversations and yet they were literally left holding the baby. That is until Mark started his campaigns. 'Yes', he was told 'of course fathers are included as part of our services' but in reality, fathers admitted to Mark that they felt they were' marginalised' 'left out of the plans' 'not considered when discussing mental health issues', 'their feelings were neglected. Fathers talked to Mark because of his rapidly increasing popularity. Mark had been there, done that, got the tee-shirt and caught the illness! He knew firsthand what it was like to watch helplessly as his wife suffered trauma. He understood how it felt be powerless to support his wife and tiny infant when they too experienced despair. He was aware that, with one or two exceptions, current National Health Services were not equipped to help him, or even acknowledge how he may be feeling. He knew he could not be alone and knew that something should be done about it. Mark generated by these events, and the love of his family, started his campaigns.

It is difficult to recollect how many times Mark and I met to discuss the next moves. Historically It was meetings in the Harvester Inns, with notepad and pen we would outline who needed to be contacted and why. Start and the top and work down to the bottom or vice versa? We knew education and training would be a good place to start. Mark's lived experience, speaking with parents and my background knowledge was an ideal recipe.

We contacted independent NHS Boards and were commissioned to do the training. We were received with great interest, practitioners were eager to learn, but and there was always a but, they did not have the resources and time. We heard that mantra for a long time until Mark said – 'then we go to the top and tell them'.

We did, and met with members of the Welsh Assembly, putting our case forward about the lack of services for parents in Wales. Some listened, some not, but those that did, including Mark Drakeford, the current First Welsh Minister, ensured that money was ringfenced for perinatal mental health services. That service, although few may recognise it, is due to the efforts of many of us, pushing, shoving and never giving up.

Mark, naturally, did not stop there. Next it was the Houses of Parliament, meeting with the members. Once again, we talked about perinatal mental health, but this time the concentration was on the mental health of fathers. Some feigned interest, others were more committed. It was, after all a new, different, and controversial area. Mark's effervescent personality ensured that this was taken seriously. Important people started to take note and there was significantly more talk about it.

Slowly more men, who were familiar with the symptoms Mark described, came forward and joined in the campaign. Some, impressed by Mark's talks and knowledge, have branched off to form companies, coalitions, and campaigns. The UK can be proud of the many services currently offered by these fathers, which are the envy of the world.

The world is another area. Mark was conscious that, amongst others, Dr Angela Barton in Canada, started the first World Maternal Mental Health Day. There was no first World Fathers' Mental Health Day until Mark founded one. He gathered experts, clinicians, practitioners, lived experience and researchers to design and develop the Day, which is held annually, to emphasise the importance of understanding and supporting fathers during this crucial period in their life.

When Mark was writing another book, I reprimanded him for not divulging and including those famous personalities he has met on his journey. There were many television appearances, meetings with royalty and with celebrities. He has the photographs and videos to prove it. Mark regularly speaks at conferences and meetings. His recent diagnosis of ADHD has inspired him to speak more widely about the condition, and he has been invited to speak at international conferences. When he finds the time, Mark has written many articles and has co-authored 2 books on perinatal mental health with me. One book is due out next Summer. Some of Mark's work was recently recognised at Westminster, where he was awarded the prestigious British Citizen Award for Health care.

Writing, like talking, does not earn fortunes. I have often rebuked Mark for subsidising the work he does, which is mostly for free. He is often on the early Mega Bus from Cardiff as it is less expensive than travelling by train, driving the length and breadth of the country to deliver his messages to a captivated audience, shaking hands with those who earn more in a day than Mark does in a year.

As if he doesn't have enough on his plate, Mark's other passion is supporting the youth in his hometown. He is revered as a football coach, youth worker and general helper when it comes to building up the self-esteem and confidence of youngsters. He also found the time to work in projects, hospitals and secure and care units.

Yet, his enthusiasm and passion remain undaunted. Mark knows he can and does make a huge difference to fathers, and to the world of perinatal mental health, and it is my honour and pleasure to have worked and to work with him in the future. Who needs fossil fuels when you have Mark?

Dr Jane Hanley Honorary Senior Lecturer, former President, and current executive member, of the International Marcé Society for Perinatal Mental Health.

Introduction

The word "trauma" is a derivative of the Greek word for "wound". This term, of course, encompasses physical, psychological, and emotional ordeals. One commonality between all types of traumas is that it interferes with the daily functioning of a person's life, sometimes to a severe degree.

I know from my own personal experience that my life is far better than it was before everything that happened, including the work I am now doing and everything I've achieved.

It was while speaking with a doctor about helping people to do what I had done in my life that I heard the words "post-traumatic growth".

Post-traumatic growth is the positive psychological change that some individuals experience after a life crisis or traumatic event. Post-traumatic growth doesn't deny deep distress, but rather posits that adversity can unintentionally yield changes in understanding oneself, others, and the world.

It was first identified by psychologists Richard Tedeschi and Lawrence Calhoun in the 1990s. Based on their research, the pair described five categories of growth that occur over time: survivors of trauma recognize and embrace new opportunities; they forge stronger relationships with loved ones as well as with victims who suffered in the same way; they cultivate inner strength through the knowledge that they have overcome tremendous hardship; they gain a deeper appreciation for life; and their relationship to religion and spirituality changes and evolves.

Trauma survivors who want to cultivate growth can strive to process the experience once they have space from it; it's nearly impossible to evolve in the middle of a crisis, but reflection in its aftermath can provide a foundation for growth. Survivors can explore how the experience changed their mindset, if they appreciate life in a new way, whether their relationships have deepened, or whether they embody a new sense of spirituality.

1

Causes of post-traumatic stress disorder (PTSD) Post-traumatic stress disorder (PTSD) is an anxiety disorder caused by very stressful, frightening, or distressing events. People who repeatedly experience traumatic situations may be diagnosed with complex PTSD.

Any situation that a person finds traumatic can cause PTSD. Serious road accidents, violent personal assaults such as sexual assault, mugging, or robbery, serious health problems, childbirth experiences. There are so many other experiences. PTSD can develop immediately after someone experiences a disturbing event, or it can occur weeks, months, or even years later.

Trigger Warning I have written in this book about some of the most horrible experiences I have witnessed and been through myself. I am also aware of that there are many things that I didn't want to share that would be horrific to read, after all its not all sunshine's and roses working in mental health.

Have you ever had someone who just didn't believe in you? Dismiss your dreams without taking the time to get to know you? Certainly, I have come across a few people over the years and often they have been professionals in sectors that we look up who feel frightened that they can't do it themselves. It is something that I have learned in my life and even though I'm at the stage in my life.

I hope you haven't bought this book to be inspired to be the next millionaire and have all the material things that some people feel will make them happy. My journey has never been about the things that come and go; it's the ripple effect to have a greater purpose in life and what has brought happiness to me.

How come a teacher told me I would never do anything with my life and wouldn't even get a job, when I have saved countless lives personally and many more each year through campaigning policies?

I didn't fail school; my school failed me. It has taken many years and since talking about my experiences in therapy I've let go off all the rubbish. Forgiveness is vital to the healing process because it allows you to let go of anger, guilt, shame, sadness, or any other feeling you may be experiencing and move on.

After finding out I had ADHD at forty years of age, I feel proud of myself how I have self-managed. I am not going to lie

2

to you, it has been hard each day but far less than it was in the early years. I have educated myself to keep the demons at bay. I have always had the ability to see the positive side of life, learning reliance along the way.

When we think of attention deficit hyperactivity disorder (ADHD), the focus is often on the deficits of the disorder. However, it's so important to recognize the many positive aspects to ADHD as well. Individuals with ADHD carry many unique capabilities that can even seem like abilities that people do not have in their lives.

Without ADHD, I would never have the creativity, ability to hyperfocus, problem solve, curiosity, charisma and most important for my own life novelty. ADHD people do not like to be bored and crave newness to keep things fresh in their lives. This has actively made me seek out new experiences, enjoying learning new ideas that are exciting and stimulating. It's certainly made me own life interesting and unique.

I have learned far more from failure than success and with hard work the aim of the book is to help you find your own purpose. There are so many people who never have the right support and direction. I am not one of those people who has just been trained to tell people that they are living their best life while showing you on adverts and this is way too way to live. I have lived it; I have worked with people who have gone through it and have seen inspirational people develop from it.

Never underestimate the magical properties of failure. It increases resilience in the face of unfavourable outcomes and gets the creative juices flowing for me anyway.

This book has been in the pipeline for nearly five years, and at many points I wanted to call it a day. I wanted something that just felt right for people and for them to get something out of it. I wanted give resources of support by signposting, which can be seen at the end of the book. The book has helped me, to write about things that I have never been able to before, to process it as well. Also, every day I am still learning and growing from it.

Be happy is worth more than gold and be what you want to be, whatever that is in your life.

Chapter 1

Childish Fears

My mother would say that I must have been having a party in her belly as I just could not keep still even during her pregnancy. So, my mum must have known she was in for a challenging time with me, and when I did manage to come out to the world on 1 August 1974 at Bridgend General Hospital, it must have been a relief.

As might be expected, my memories of the 1970s are rather sketchy. After all, I was only four years of age at the turn of the last decade, so I look back with the eyes of a young child. But I do remember my first memory of going to school, which for me was crying to my mother on a cold wet morning in October.

If you were brought up in the seventies, you'll know that it seems like a totally different world back then than it does today. The three channels of the television set were then comfortable and considered enough.

The memory of setting foot into my mother's car while she warmed her hands at the wheel, wiping the windscreen to clear her view to drive while asking me if I was alright, giving me that sense of security, warmed me up inside as it was so cold in the back of the car; it was traumatizing, in fact. I didn't want to leave and was happy in my environment.

As my mother drove to the local nursery, I could hear her say, "Mark, give it a go, you'll be fine." I didn't take much confidence with her warm friendly words, as I didn't know what was ahead.

The second thing I remember is seeing the playground as I approached this bungalow-looking building which took my mind instantly away from the feeling of numbness in my toes, or maybe they were too numb to feel—I don't know.

As we both entered the building, I remember being greeted by my teacher as my hand slipped slowly away from my mother's and into the hand of my teacher, experiencing these overwhelming feelings of despair and uncertainty. As I could see a rocking horse in the background, these feelings of fear of having to stay at nursery left instantly.

It was not long until I was rocking away like some cowboy, not noticing my mother's hands waving goodbye as she headed back to the car. I was in a moment of pleasure until I heard a clip of the hands from the teacher and was told to sit quietly on the floor. I just wanted to play and explore the room that was now like a new adventure to me.

Nursery was a place where you could learn and play with other children before entering primary school and being an only child—yes, an only child, not a lonely child. It was a fundamental way to mix with other children of my own age. I explore freely and take risks which are something we tend to lose as we grow older.

The other memories are of running in a summer race without a care in the world and coming first, which certainly gave me attention from the other children. The three-legged races and egg-and-spoon races would give me the same attention as I landed straight on my face in front of a crowd; they weren't my best moments. But they taught me to get up from the dirt and do better next time.

The playground was a magical place for a child. Climbing the trees gave me a sense of achievement, where most of the children hesitated. There was the excitement of the swinging bars and slides, and after my go, I would try to patiently wait my turn, which wasn't always easy for me.

I had no fear or insight into danger, which of course resulted in accidents and being hurt. The cuts and bruises piled up, with the occasional visit to the hospital with my frustrated parents. It didn't matter what they said to me; I had no fear of danger and was just feeling happy looking for my next adventure.

Apart from the activities, I can't remember if I ever struggled with the education side. I can't remember ever being shouted at in nursery. I felt I had settled in quickly and made friends which helped boost my confidence and self-esteem. The teachers encouraged me to give it a chance and talked to me in a way that I could relate to.

As a child, the days seemed so much longer, while the summers seemed to be way brighter and sunnier than I can remember today. It didn't really matter anyway what the weather was like; it could be raining, snowing, thunder, and lightning, I would still be in our garden tapping the football against the wall.

I have since realized as time has gone by that sometimes the simplest things in life can bring you the most enjoyment, as I learned once again during the pandemic.

The memory from the 1970s that sticks in the corners of my mind with clarity is of the power cuts—on several occasions I can recall the entire house turning black without warning and my mum and dad's mad rush to search out the candles in the pantry. After the initial shock at suddenly finding oneself in the pitch dark, the power cuts were a novel way to spend the evening.

It was fun and exciting. I loved the flickering candlelight and the way we all sat together until the lights came back on. With a candle nearby we would get the catalogue out to look at the toys. As a family we tended to see what goofy things we could do in a bit situation.

I loved my grandmother – I loved all my grandparents so much. My grandmother was very old school and, of course, she learned from her mother. There was a strong church community back in those days. One time she ran after me and caught me after I'd said a swear word and quickly washed out my mouth with a bar of soap. I never, ever swore in front of my grandmother again.

If I had something in my hands and something to stimulate me, I was fine, no outbursts, no tantrums. I was content. It was quite a simple life and my family always tried to get me involved in something. One of the things I remember is that Grandmother would take me on the bus to pick up the adults who had disabilities and autism. People who had been sheltered away from society and had limited options than others were the kindest of people.

These wonderful people would later make me a wooden castle which I used just as much as any other toy I was given. I would spend hours just playing soldiers and trying to hit the soldiers down with marbles. I remember how so many talented, caring people were treated unfairly, and being around them gave me empathy when children could be so unkind.

I would become very creative in my play; I would make anything out of nothing, and Blue Peter, the television programme had an influence on me of course. With little money available, I collected waste and turned it into something that could keep me occupied for hours.

My first sense of fear was getting ready for change at primary school, where this time the building looked scary and haunted. The school was an old, Victorian building. The only benefit of the school was that it was sited near my grandparents' house. The conversation again started with, "Mum, I don't want to go," and after finishing yet another bowl of porridge I again had no choice.

As I entered the gates, it seemed overwhelming, much more than nursery school with more people attending all at once. The calls to my mother to let me go home were in vain; and anyway, I could see I was not getting out of this one. Funny how I can't remember much from the month before, but I have a vivid memory of my first teacher.

The large, framed windows and walls towered over me, as over thirty children cramped into the class waiting to start. I didn't know anyone from nursery school for some reason; they all went to the primary school down the road. The horrible feeling of leaving my mother's hand didn't leave this time and I noticed her wave to say her goodbyes.

"Everyone who is incapable of learning has taken to teaching." – Oscar Wilde

I soon realized this would be different as, if we were naughty, we were made to stand in the corner or face the wall. Some of the things that labelled me as being naughty were forgetting things, over talking, and being active in the class and being told that this was classed as bad behaviour.

I can certainly understand the frustration it brought to the teacher, but the things I could not control made me feel even more anxious, as I knew I would be punished. The chat to other children was shut down with a raw and I was told to be quiet. This I could not understand as in nursery school this was

7

encouraged; after all, some of the best skills to have has to be communication and listening skills.

Losing my school bag and items that were needed for school was a consent battle. It was not as if I was doing it for attention; and after all, it wasn't good for me, knowing my parents did not have a great deal of money. I tried and the more I thought about the situation the more anxious I would become.

When I had my school bag at hand, my bag was always disorganized, and I would spend more time inside my head trying to work out the things that I needed. I felt I was checking my pockets all the time in case I lost my money.

It was not the ideal start to school in my first year, but I found things settled down as again I started to focus on breaktimes and a chance to play sport in the school grounds. It was a time to be free-minded and not controlled and play new games with excitement.

It certainly wasn't anything that I meant to do, and it made me worry. I believe to this day that there is always something behind a child's bad behaviour, and a better way to deal with it is to explore why it is happening, rather than just shouting, and screaming at them.

I was now struggling with classes and my speech wasn't good. It was now being picked up that I needed speech therapy, which my parents gladly engaged in with the school. I was then put in what was called a special class, with other children, for reading. These classes were looked down upon by other children and it came across as though we were not as bright.

For years it was missed that I had dyslexia which I thought only happens when words start popping out of the book. This was not the case for me. I didn't know until I researched it years later that there are many forms of dyslexia, like Double Deficit Dyslexia, Phonological Dyslexia, Rapid Automatic Naming Dyslexia, Surface Dyslexia, Visual Dyslexia, Primary Dyslexia, among others.

A lot of dyslexia research uses a type of brain scan called MRI. Scans are used for different purposes. Some look at brain structure. Others look at brain function associated with a task (like reading). And some measure the brain's chemistry. n all of these areas, researchers have seen differences between people who have dyslexia and those who don't.

For example, the parts of the brain involved in reading don't function the same in people with dyslexia as they do in others. Functional MRI (fMRI) scans show that some areas are less active. That can make it hard for people with dyslexia to learn to read.

Dyslexia may run in families. As many as 49 percent of parents of kids with dyslexia also have it. And about 40 percent of siblings will also struggle with reading.

Researchers have also been looking at specific genes. So far, they've found several genes that are linked to reading and language processing issues. These genes likely play slightly different roles. Some are thought to impact brain development. Others are thought to impact how the brain communicates. So, your child's reading difficulties probably aren't due to just one gene.

My writing was not bad, and people could understand it, certainly in primary school. I would even write on my hand to remind me of things to do. There were certain subjects that my writing was better in, as I remember writing who were my heroes, and of course that was a subject about my parents which I had a lot to say about.

I found my English and writing was better when I was focused on something that I enjoyed, and it is the same today. Passion comes out and my creativity is better than writing about something that doesn't get my attention.

When there was little understanding, of course, this didn't help my self-esteem and it was a case of just carrying on with no professional support. Sadly, for me, this makes you feel that you're not as intelligent as the other children in the class. Their other issue was that throughout my schooling life, sometimes I couldn't take in the information from the teacher.

It just went In and out of my mind, whether I was interested in the subject or not, while trying hard to keep still in case I was shouted at. This increased my anxiety, which again would be released with my friends in the playground.

Throughout my time in primary school, I was not bullied and fortunately there was no social media back then. The only time I had experienced name-calling was when I tried riding down a coal tip and headed over the handlebars. I had a cut above my lip and needed stiches.

Coal dust entered the cut, so it looked like I had a small moustache. I didn't find the comments very helpful but just laughed it off. Being the class joker was part of my schooling. I was the one that people could laugh at and it made me feel included.

I would have this tic where I would stretch my neck and could not stop blinking. Another one I have today when I think about it is making little sounds with the back of my mouth while blinking one eye. It is so hard to control it. These tics would become more intense the more anxious I became, and I just couldn't get the thoughts out of my mind. I felt better after doing them. I was experiencing spasm-like movements of muscles.

But the worst I remember is the one type of muscle twitch which I now know is called "benign essential blepharospasm". Blepharospasm refers to the muscles of one or both eyelids twitching uncontrollably. This occurred repeatedly and I cannot remember when it finished. I am sure I had it during my working life as well.

I felt that being involved with classmates was important and it made me the person I am today. We would engage in gambling with marbles, and if I won, I would earn a few pence selling them back. It was all mischief fun and never hurt anyone. I think I learned more from the playground about life in general than any classroom could offer.

As I was entering the last year of primary school, the one lesson I enjoyed was Maths. I like to think I am still good at numbers even today. It was the one lesson apart from physical education that gripped me with passion. I don't know if there is something about numbers that makes me feel more comfortable than with words.

My school reports apart from for Mathematics and Physical Education in primary had always been poor. They were always something like, Mark is always daydreaming and can be lazy in class. That envelope we had off the teacher would fill me with dread, but my parents didn't really get to upset with me, and I certainly can't remember them shouting at me with the results. Perhaps they realized that, like them, school just was not for me.

I think what hurt was that there was not anyone sitting me down to explain how people like me could improve; and after all, there is always a reason behind someone's behaviours.

In the last days of term, before the summer holiday, there might be that one saint of a teacher who decided that they were going to deliver the lesson on the playing field. This was like a luxury and a day from sitting still behind the desk staring at the four walls.

Listening to stories when everyone was quiet, enjoying the sun and the fresh air seemed like everything was in the moment. No loud noises from in front or behind from the children in the class helped me to focus once again. I could stretch out and stand up while listening to the teacher and visualize the story in my head. We weren't closed in and told not to move at the desks.

"How I hated schools, and what a life of anxiety I lived there. I counted the hours to the end of every term, when I should return home. I always like to learn, but I don't always like to be taught." – Winston Churchill

Somehow again life seemed simpler then. After all, it would be a while before the ever-increasing amounts of technology bombarded the leisure time of children. I remember my first feelings of independence as I took the glass bottles back to the local shop and yes, recycling, which is often considered a new thing in recent years due to climate change.

Bottles were reused back then, and you were given a small amount for your troubles. You could still buy sweets for a penny (in fact, some even cost half a penny, and we still had the tiny, light half-pence coins). Buying our own sweets in the corner shop was a simple pleasure and was enough to make us happy.

There wasn't much media attention of the bad people in life. I still can picture the day as clear as yesterday. I was walking back from my grandparents' when a car pulled up on the other side of the road. I was with a friend and was around eight years old. The driver pulled down his window and shouted over, "Hi both, your father asked me to pick you up."

I remember that his accent was totally different. He seemed calm and talked politely to us. As I walked towards the car, I explained that I only lived nearby as I pointed to what he thought was the house near us, and in fact it was five minutes as the crow flies.

As he looked at us, he looked at the house and shot off in a hurry. It was only as time has gone by that I have reflected on this time and have over thought where I would be today if in that split second, I didn't say what I did and instead went right up to the man who knows what may have happened.

This has come up a lot in some of my dreams and when the friend passed away at a young age, it made me think why my school friend never went out after leaving school and was totally homebound. We didn't have a conversation ever in school after that day, but it has made me think that we are all of seconds away from any life-changing event.

During the last few years of primary school, my parents introduced me to the youth club. I had already enrolled in judo and cub scouts, while the local swimming pool was open back then so every hour of the day after school and the weekend, I was letting off steam being active. I was never in the house and if there were no sports to do, it was a case of playing until the streetlights came on, as that was the sign that it was time to go home.

It was life-changing meeting Stan "the man" Norris MBE, who in over fifty years had voluntarily helped so many young people in our community. It was Stan who had seen a talent in me and pushed me to take sport more seriously.

The club had everything I needed. I tried sports that I had never experienced before. The club was two houses knocked into one and, at the time, cost £1 for a year's membership and 10p admission. From day one I loved the place and being around different people. I made lifelong friends.

There were some characters like Walter, who had learning difficulties and always call me Martin. He helped Stan raise money by selling the valley raffle tickets each week. Stan gave Walter a purpose and was a big part of the club.

Then there was Spider, who helped Stan on a Thursday and showed us how to play table tennis. He always made us laugh and he put us right if we did anything wrong; he talked to us to make us understand better. Spider loved the club like the rest of community, who all worked there voluntarily after a long day down the mines.

Billy was the table-tennis coach. Twenty kids who wanted to play on one table made it fun; we had to run to the back of the queue after our go and we were knocked out if we missed a shot. Billy was my coach, and I even came second in the Welsh championships for my age group.

My parents always had my back and wanted the best for me, but Stan pushed me to enter competitions in all sports, explaining to me that you should never listen to people who are knocking you down and you should only listen to the ones who fully understand you as a person. Stan took the time, where the teachers could only see my behaviours. That good self-esteem at that time was critical, and as comprehensive school was approaching, I knew I had something to look forward to and that was sport.

Sport gave me so much and brought the community together. The people became more friendly, even outside that community. Sport was and still is my happy go-to place where I go to forget about everything troubling me. I remember having my first BMX bike and how it just changed my life at that point. I was the bees' knees with my bike helmet and knee pads.

I was trying my best to be like the rest of my mates who were good at doing white lines on the main road, trying to wheelie as far as possible. I think I made up by the fact I wasn't scared and did not know danger.

I just loved music, and I always will. With music, nothing else matters. It is meditation, in its purest form. The melodies seep into my mind, washing away worries and doubts. But back then records were expensive and bootlegging music existed in the '80s, too, it just involved sitting next to the radio and waiting for the local station to play your favourite tune, all while resting one finger on the record button of your cassette player.

Researchers found that music releases dopamine, the feel-good chemical in your brain. It also found that dopamine was up to 9% higher when volunteers listened to music that they enjoyed. It may be obvious to us, but it is strong evidence for the link between music and mental wellbeing.

I loved making wooden ramps and jumping as far as I could, which wasn't as far as I would often land and harm myself, but I just jumped back on and tried again. We found comfort in making things out of nothing, whether that was cabins in the woods or dams to jump into near the river by our house.

Throughout the final year I must have dodged more dust board dusters and items like chalks being thrown at me by the teachers than in my entire primary school years. I laugh about it now; it made my kickboxing skills better because of all that dodging. However, it wasn't pleasant to have your knuckles hit by rulers, or your sideburns pulled by the teacher, or to be threatened with the cane and having to wait outside the headmaster's room.

The cane was always in sight of the headmaster's room, and he always made you aware that it was there. I remember one child got tied to his chair with a skipping rope by the teacher because he would not sit still.

Perhaps the most popular choice (with the teachers!) was 100 lines on several pieces of lined paper that the teacher had given you. During the school break I would occasionally find myself repeatedly writing and quoting that I must not throw paper airplanes across the classroom as it.

Many of us used our out-of-the-box thinking to put two pens together to write the hundred lines faster than just having one pen. The teacher would find out and give us more lines rather than encourage our creativity.

Writing these lines seemed an eternity and then we'd hand them in only for the teacher to screw them up into a tight ball and simply throw them into the bin. All your hard work was destroyed in an instant.

Some of the things that I would be shouted at for was clicking my pen in class which I just did not notice, and if there was no pen in my hand there would be constant tapping. I would be listening for one minute and under the desk looking for the bubble gum. I was so easily distracted, and it was getting me in trouble by no fault of my own. I tried so hard to concentrate, but it was exhausting, and it was better just to go with the flow.

The fear that it brought and the punishment which was handed out by teachers was far worse than in my home. My parents were always setting firm boundaries and telling me the difference between right and wrong, mostly for coming in late after the streetlights came on.

School was something different and the punishment would involve being picked up under your armpits and pinned to the wall. To think that hitting a child by a parent is now labelled abuse, but back than it was a daily thing that happened and destroyed many children.

It was not just the physical side of the punishment that hurt; it was the words that were spoken too. Words do hurt. Ridicule, disdain, humiliation, and taunting all cause injury, and when it is delivered from childhood friends, verbal abuse causes more than emotional trauma. It inflicts lasting physical effects on brain structure.

Words can be so harmful when you have someone telling you on a regular basis and shouting out in front of the whole class, "Can you do anything right?" or "Are you not listening again Mark?" They didn't think that maybe it was because of how they taught, and it could have been the frustration that had built up in their private lives that was released on to us children.

When the teacher did talk about something I was interested in and I tried to put my point across, I was quickly shut down and told to be quiet. There was no two-way conversation, and I was never asked if there was anything I could add to the lesson.

"I remember that I was never able to get along at school. I was at the foot of the class." – Thomas Edison

We know the power of the spoken word, and when it is said in a positive way it can help your own mental health. Our thoughts also impact what we manifest in our lives. But it can be argued that the real power lies in our words. It is our words that provide a bold affirmation of our innermost thoughts.

It is confirmation to the world of how we see others, our lives, and ourselves. The power of words can build self-esteem, and the message that if someone isn't listened to can be put across in better tone body language. Maybe the teachers could have put it across in front of the class as more, "Mark, let's give it go together," or maybe, "Mark, you okay with that, or anyone need me to go over it again?" or, "Maybe we can work on that in a different way, Mark."

The one thing that all children looked forward to, had to be summertime break. Like most children, we counted down the days to be free and outside. It was a time to play in the mountains, while building cabins and river dams. Those six weeks were like heaven, and we didn't waste any days inside. I just could not be stuck inside the house, and with a football under my feet it was time to have fun.

As we were all in the same place, I don't think any of us ever asked for much in childhood; there was no pressure to have the latest designer clothing. The sounds of the birds and the wind blowing in our faces gave us the sense of freedom we needed in our childhoods.

The years went past, and my confidence grew in the play yard. I was involved in the basketball team, and I loved playing against other schools. The rugby on the other hand didn't go that well and was totally terrible. I would be talking to my friend on the rugby posts while the other teams scored the tries.

This was not great for the coach who was an ex-player and took the job seriously. I just didn't enjoy playing the game and was more for the round ball. Football was encouraged, but there was no team in primary school, so it was rugby or nothing if there were no basketball matches.

Due to the strictness of the teacher, so many tried to get out of playing rugby, including myself in the end. The physical and mental punishment if we dropped the ball or were not listening to the instructions given to us was cruel. After all, I was only ten years of age and to be treated like that in front of everyone was shameful.

It was something that has stuck with me years later when I decided to coach football to young players; the most important thing about playing the sport is to enjoy and encourage. To be a good role model, to set them up as a leader of people in whatever part they play in society. Not to knock the stuffing out of someone for doing something wrong.

The last year of primary was not the greatest. It was spent either standing outside the headmaster's door or feeling like I was going to be punished at any time during the class. I wasn't looking forward to going to comprehensive school in the coming months, but I looked at it as a year closer to getting out of school, even at that age.

When children are exposed to disturbing stories, images, or videos, they may find it difficult to process and cope with distressing stimuli. This may lead children to struggle with fear, anxiety, aggression, sleeping problems, and behavioural difficulties (Wang et al., 2006). One study suggests that watching just five minutes of distressing news daily can lead to these types of secondary traumatic stress symptoms in preschool-aged children (Wang et al., 2006).

Sadly, our lives would change in the same year, as 6 March 1984 would be the start of the miners' strike. It was the first time I could see my family feel anger as their world was unravelling. The strike affected the whole community, and my father, uncles, and grandfathers were all coal miners, making us heavily involved in the tough times ahead.

The problem with the eighties was that it was a time of contrasts. Half of the country seemed to be booming and the other half was bust and ignored. If you lived in one of the more prosperous areas, then life was good. People ignored other people's suffering, and as children our environment can be just as traumatizing as being a place of fear.

One benefit was seeing more of my father. He would sometimes go on the picket lines late at night to support the miners on strike. This helped him give him some purpose in his life. It also helped with his need to bring some money into the home. It was only a few pounds if he was lucky, but it was a sense of achievement and that he was doing something to stand up to the people who were trying to take his love of work away.

I have memories of going to the pantomimes and the meals which were given to all the miners' children, and everyone came together as a community once again.

The miners' wives came into their own with their effective campaign to back their men's cause. South Wales was one of the most solid areas to hold the strike. I always remember my great grandparents shouting in front of the television at the prime minister which was something I had never seen. The images on television of the fights on the picket lines, knowing my father may be going one night, were unsettling.

These memories shape my thinking even today. It was being around people who were struggling just to put food on the table. For those who lived in areas which depended on industry, however, things were very different. While areas of the country lost their key sources of income and with it the very social fabric holding society together, coal mining, steel works, and other heavy industries in Wales reduced and disappeared. Those communities affected have, to this day, never recovered, nor have they forgiven those who left them as broken people. In the communities, life would never be the same again.

These memories have made me the person I am today, and it shows how something in your life which is out of your control can be the downfall; many families were now on the breadlines and going to soup kitchens and having food parcels delivered to the door.

It was around this time I started to shoplift and steal sweets from the big stores in the town. With friends we would come up with plans to get past the security guard at the front door by distracting him. I knew it was wrong of course and I only worried that my family would find out which scared me far more than the police.

After many months of stealing and getting more confident at what I was doing I was starting to steal bigger things. Trying to hide these items from my family was hard. I was even questioned by my friend's family; in reply we said we had found some money on the floor and spent it.

It was at Woolworths, a national store which has now gone from the high streets, that I would get caught red-handed. It was there by a security guard as I was putting an item in my pocket that he told me in my ear, "You're not going to pay for that, are you? I would put it back." The feelings of being caught and my parents finding out hit me like a ton of bricks.

As I slowly put the items back, I headed towards the door and the feelings of being shamed would have such an impact on me that I would never steal from anyone ever again. I was never afraid of the police; it was more of what my family would think of me.

After all, some people in the community hated the police for what they used to say to the miners while on the picket lines, gloating over the money they were earning from overtime. Flashing the cash in front of people who could not put food on the table for their young children. I never heard my father say anything bad about the police, after all his cousins and uncle was actually high up in the South Wales police force.

Honest hardworking men would steal coal just to warm the homes in the winter, and they were shamed into thinking they weren't good enough by the people who should have been protecting them and were looked up to into society.

"I remember that I was never able to get along at school. I was at the foot of the class." – Thomas Edison

Chapter 2

Lost in Battle

It was then I started playing football at under 12s level and just loved it. Stan would often ask me to play for the older team at under 16s level if they were short of numbers in the afternoon. Those days made me, and that certainly wouldn't happen today playing on ice-frozen pitches with no shin pads, but it made my character.

To be around older children and learn what they were doing as they were about to leave school and earn money gave me ideas to do something while I could. I had already had a paper round from the age of ten years, but I wanted to earn more money.

I started with a friend during the summer doing a window cleaning round on the weekends and was earning more in one day than a whole week as a paperboy. I enjoyed the conversations with the elderly who were so grateful as we were very cheap compared to professionals, but they were always satisfied.

It was my first business and it taught me that you can start with nothing and earn your own money rather than earn money for other people. What I found earning money it was something for myself, that give me my first experience of working unsupervised and independently.

"I have never let my schooling interfere with my education." –Mark Twain

After the summer of 1984, it was near the time to start comprehensive school. Before school started again in September, I went to Woolworths or WH Smith to buy brand-new stationery, all paid for this time, and ended up losing it within the first week.

The school was far worse than primary school. It was even more crowded, as all the primary schools came together. Some of the pupils we had fought against in rugby were now all together trying to settle disagreements in those in the first few weeks. After those weeks we all became friends.

One of my first memories was covering school exercise books in 1980s wallpaper, which was the one thing back at secondary school. Not cool, marble print… We're talking garishly bad floral designs. At school, sometimes the teacher would ask you to re-write something in red, or green, or make changes in a different colour. To save space, everyone would have one of those chunky pens that could change colour with a simple click.

Once again, I was put in a class for my reading and writing. The school was an old building with wooden desks full of bubble gum and of course I put my own artistic spin on them. The lessons again didn't interest me and sometimes the teacher's tone would make you feel tired and bored.

I will always remember the joy of watching television, seeing the TV being wheeled into the classroom, knowing that you will be spending the whole lesson watching a programme on the subject that we were talking about in class. I took in information better by images and connected these images to the answers.

That beautiful sound of hearing three bells, signalling a 'wet' break. And what did wet break mean…? Chaos in the corridor. With no mobiles then we created our own fun. This sometimes was a game of trying to get the coin across the desk to the end and then flip the coin to catch it and score. We gambled our dinner money by throwing coins at nearest to the wall.

I really enjoyed woodwork lessons because they were an opportunity to express my artistic side, although woodwork really wasn't my thing. Nonetheless, every week I would waste a couple of hours working on utterly useless items for use around the home.

Cookery lessons gave me the opportunity to stand up and walk around the classroom. I love art now and do a lot of street photography, graffiti on cardboard, but it just didn't interest me doing a papier-mâché mask, blowing up a balloon and gluing paper to it.

The older teachers were reluctant to use the newer eighties' teaching methods. It seemed to a young lad that they refused to move out of the sixties and seventies, Bryl cream, thinning hair and wearing seventies-style sideburns with large-collared shirts. They would also call me, in a patronizing manner, by my surname. They just didn't connect to us and that no have a go at the way they dressed, but they didn't seem update if that makes sense.

Then there was assembly; the thought of standing in front of everyone and being called to the front was scary for me. One of things I tried to avoid was speaking in front of the entire school.

As school budgets were slashed, hymn books were instead replaced with overhead projectors and the words written on acetate sheets which were then beamed onto screens, often with much focus required. All the greats were included— "All Things Bright and Beautiful", "Onward Christian Soldiers", and "Give Me Joy in My Heart"—for those sat cross-legged on the cold, wooden hall floor.

My father was now back at work as the miners' strike ended after a whole year. It was such a relief to see how happy my family were. My father now had a purpose to get up in the morning and go to work to provide for his family.

The mines later closed down+, and the mining community dissolved with the government not meeting the needs of employment for many people. The mining community had such an influence on society and had first-hand experience of social injustice.

One of them was the alliances which the campaign forged between the lesbian, gay, bisexual, and transgender (LGBT) community and British Labour groups, which proved to be an important turning point in the progression of LGBT issues in the United Kingdom. Miners' Labour groups began to support, endorse, and participate in various gay pride events throughout the UK, including leading the London Lesbian and Gay Pride parade in 1985.

Additionally, at the 1985 Labour Party conference in Bournemouth, a resolution committing the party to the support of LGBT rights passed, due to block-voting support from the National Union of Mineworkers. The miners' groups were also among the most outspoken allies of the LGBT community in the 1988 campaign against Section 28.

Only in recent years we have become more aware of equality, diversity, and inclusion, tackling all forms of discrimination, and fostering good relationships between diverse groups of people in society. I sometimes wonder why it is mentioned as I see the person and understand that there are people who don't have the same views as me.

After the miners' strike, my family decided to take a holiday to Malta. It had been a year of hell in our community and now things were getting back to normal. After a few days on the island, we decided to take a day trip into the capital. It was a bright sunny day, and the temperature was very high.

We walked down a street where a few people were looking in the shops. What happened in the next few seconds seemed to be in slow motion. My uncle was many yards away when suddenly a wave of people came rushing down the street. One moment we could see my uncle and the next we could not as he disappeared in the crowd.

The crowd hit us like a wave. My father pushed me and my mother towards a doorway. All I could see was the sun disappear and arms everywhere. My father told me to stay there. He could see my uncle. He was on the ground as he pushed himself towards us. My father grabbed his hand and, using all his strength, managed to get him out of the crowd.

My uncle couldn't catch his breath and could not get any air. He was shaking after what had happened in a split second. It was only then that I started to realise that my uncle had never been comfortable with going to new places and getting into lifts. It was lucky for him that the mines closed, and he never had to go down in a cage again. He suffered panic attacks, and that day truly affected his mental health and confidence.

For many years I didn't understand why my uncle was behaving the way he did and avoided situations. After all, when I wanted to go somewhere I just went. It was something we never talked about until in recent years. It was a shame; with professional support my uncle might have lived more happier life when exploring the things that we take for granted.

After some research about that period in Malta, I found that in the 1980s most minority groups there were struggling, even though benefits and pensions were offered in abundance. The economy was dreary and mind-numbing. As in George Orwell's book 1984, 'Peace, plenty, love and truth' seemed to have a completely different meaning from that in dictionaries.

The eighties were a time when the church and the government were in collusion from morning till night. Some people believe that Malta was on the brink of civil war. My experience took place on the day that the Pope's assistant had shown up in Valetta; even now, as I write this part of the book, I can clearly see the doorway my father put me in for safety and the sea of heads above me. Some things are just stored away until we start thinking about them.

In the '80s, the only way to interact with friends was face-to-face, in real time, usually on the playground. Instead of depending on texts, Twitter DMs, or Snapchat, your friends were people that you knew and saw daily. You joked with them, had conflicts with them, and made memories with them—all while experiencing fresh air and making eye contact in the community. I have since learned there is a place for technologies and times move on but being part of the community, I am pretty sure helped my mental health back then.

Today, having your own computer is more of a necessity than a privilege. But in the '80s, when computers were becoming more widely available to people who weren't scientists in lab coats, we were blown away every time we got to so much as play with one. Some of us were lucky enough to own our own Commodore 64, or like me a dragon 32 which later went bust.

The games would take ages to load and then crush. I would become so angry when this would happen. It was a simple game of football management that took me in. With posters in my bedroom and the match of the day on a Saturday night, I just loved the game.

I played football every chance that I had, and it took away all the stress of being in school. I was addicted to football and started watching the game on television with my father. That was rare back then. After the miners' strike, when my father was made redundant after twenty-six years in the mines, I went to my first football match.

We would pick up sandwiches from the sandwich shop, jump on a train that still had the old-style carriages and talk all the way there. My father even took me to Wembley when Maradona was playing in a friendly game. After seeing him live, he became one of my heroes. Many young boys dreamed of playing at Wembley. Unable to play on football pitches in the winter, we made goalposts out of clothes on the road at the back of my house.

I always felt older than my age and the club helped me become more streetwise. I learned life skills that gave me the confidence to explore outside the valley. I think the furthest place my grandparents on my father's side had gone in their lives was Weston-Super-Mare, which was two hours down the road. That was normal back then.

Around this time, I met my brother from another mother, Elward, and him being two and half years older than me was not a factor in our friendship. He looked after me and even after over thirty-five years plus of friendship still is there for me when I need anything. Having a few close friends, like Elward is enough for me. That feeling that you would do anything for him and the way he felt for me is so close that nothing now can be broken.

If you have amazing people you can trust in your life, you're lucky and I am certainly that when it comes to them.

I started playing pool, table tennis, and even running cross country for the club, and my fitness back then was so good, I feel it was one of the reasons I got on well with our Physical Education teacher. He was an old traditional schoolteacher, but if you give him 100 per cent in sport, he engaged with you so much better. I was never going to compete in the next Olympics, and maybe if I had focused on just one sport, I could have gone so much further.

They say that children with conduct disorders are violating rules, stealing, breaking, and entering, and skipping school, but looking back, so many people were doing the same. Additionally, the symptoms of conduct disorders can be mild, moderate, or severe. My own opinion is that that may we have to look at the environment.

I just didn't see any danger of climbing 140 feet telephone masts. I nearly slipped just running across the road with no sense of danger from oncoming traffic. If I was asked to do something as a dare, I was the first to put my hand up, and that caused injury most of the time.

I was so impulsive, living for the day and making the best to enjoy ourselves. I can't think of anything that we didn't do and of course football was a big part of it back then. If the football pitches were waterlogged, we would jump over the fence in the school and play there until being chased from the caretaker.

"The only source of knowledge is experience." – Albert Einstein

I always had a good work ethic which was instilled in me from a young age. That was also ingrained in my father, by my grandfather. Work hard and play hard on the weekends was often heard throughout. I was told that whatever I wanted to do, whether it was a cleaner or the top job in the mines: "Do it well and you be alright in life."

I remember my father telling me that he would be so proud if I played for Wales. I always wanted to play football at any level. I was fourteen and captain of our football team, and I had the game of my life when we played our rivals who were the league champions.

We won the game 2–1. The coach, who was also a county coach, came into our changing rooms and told me in front of everyone else, 'You will go far if you keep trying.' Looking back, I was never going to be a professional footballer at the highest level, but I was good enough to be capped at schoolboy level for Wales and maybe who knows play non-league football.

When the trials came around, I was so disappointed that I was too old by one month because my birthday was in August. In my local team I saw players who we were beating every time get into the national team and I knew I was better than them. So, I quit and didn't play competitive football until I started work years later. The reason I quit was disappointment because I wanted to wear the national shirt and make my father proud. When I think back, he was always proud of me as long as I earned my way in life and was happy.

That is something that I did, and I became a British champion in my sport after leaving football. The hard work had paid off and that shaped me in my life, that when you put all your effort into something anyone can be successful.

Representing our country was something that no one could take away from us and to eventually win the British Championship was something that I could make my parents proud of. I had always wanted to wear my country colours and after that goal was done, my training just went downhill rapidly.

I was now starting the weekends at house parties, drinking. Even while training and at school I would have a Saturday night only drinking at the bus stop but now it was Friday and Saturdays.

Now it was the start of the nineties, and it was exciting how things were changing in everything, from the start of the Premier League to the UK's grunge chart-takeover of the early nineties which created a backlash in the form of Britpop. I just loved the music scene, and with the rave scene now hitting new heights I fitted in well.

I would travel all over the place: Manchester, London, and other parts of the United Kingdom. I was independent at a young age and street wise. I started going to concerts as well as football matches at fifteen with my friends. I grew in confidence and travelling anywhere I had never been before just didn't bother me.

Throughout school, teachers often asked me to participate in group projects. It usually went something like this: Three less-motivated classmates would pair up with the smart person and let the smart kid do all the work. These motivationally changed kids would then ascribe their names to the project to get credit. This was something that I would find out years later, working in mental health. The less-motivated kids like me would always give something to the project but would not get the credit they would deserve.

I was hardly there at all during the last year of school; I was just skipping school and when my name was called out in class for registration, one of my friends would say "Yes" or "Yeah", and of course I did the same for them as well.

With school coming to an end, I was told to just bring a book or magazine to classes so I would not disturb the other children.

I was not alone; I was with school mates who were put in the corner of the class away from the rest.

So, it was no surprise that I ended school with nothing to show for it. Not one pass in my exams, which was expected as I was not put through to them leaving school at fifteen years of age.

As a signing off and a tick box exercise I was asked to go to see the careers advisor, and I walked into the room with a teacher who had put many of us down and was very disliked among us. The careers officer was the teacher.

He was that teacher that would have a major impact on my life and fire in my belly when he told me, "Williams, you will never get a job or do anything with your life." I remember exactly where I was and what I was wearing when he said that, even after all these years.

Isn't it sad that one person can have a major impact and ripple effect on so many lives. I was lucky to see through him and think to myself that I had two jobs and had just won a British Championship, and he was telling me at fifteen that I would never do anything with my life.

Over the years I have often reflected on that teacher who never laid a single finger on me compared to some teachers who could have done the most damage mentally if I didn't have the foundations and had witnessed trauma in my childhood within my home which home was the place that made me safe.

How dare someone make matters worse for other people, especially when they've chosen to work in a field which is supposed to be there to support that person. I have worked with many people in later life and there are some people who have no empathy and understanding.

These people should be brought to attention and not just be able to provide their glamourized CV and get work doing something that has influence over people who need that help. The determination and tenacity to never give in to negativity is key and changing our communication style can make a huge difference to the cultural identity of a school. 'We first' is important because the focus is on everyone and not just the pupils. Everyone matters and everyone must participate, contribute, and learn in an atmosphere that offers positive solutions.

Schools can be stressful places that make people not talk freely and show their emotions if they act outside the norm. Places with negative people in charge can breed negative thinking and toxicity. When left unchecked, the moans and groans can become embedded in a school's culture and quickly become part of the fabric. This negativity and stress can also be contagious and passed onto children, so it needs to be addressed quickly.

At fifteen I left school with the feeling of being free from the anxiety that it had caused, without any qualifications.

Chapter 3

Breathing Blue

Now I felt I could make my own choices at last and was excited about entering the real world. That was a big transition, leaving school at fifteen and then working, but I just wanted to work. There was no internet and, with some companies you not could legally work until the age of sixteen, so I went cold-calling around the factories on an industrial estate.

After walking around the trading estate factories and knocking on doors, I was offered a job making medical equipment in a dusty old warehouse. I didn't last long as they found out I was only fifteen, and I left after two days and signed up for the YTS the following week.

The Youth Training Scheme was founded around the 1981 England riots that brought into sharp focus the results of large numbers of unskilled unemployed finding their own solutions.

The scheme was first outlined in the 1980 white paper "A New Training Initiative: A Program for Action", and it was brought into operation in 1983 to replace the Youth Opportunities Programme by the government of Margaret Thatcher. Initially lasting one year or six months, the scheme was amended in 1986 to be so that it could be extended to two years.

The scheme promised training to its applicants and made use of a variety of different training locales such as businesses, colleges of further education or training workshops run by voluntary organizations. Since the training place was guaranteed by the Government and trainees were to be paid if they were on the course, eligibility for unemployment benefit was withdrawn.

It was known as the Young, think and stupid scheme (YTS) I signed up for bricklaying and never laid a brick, and I painted an old run-down community hall.

I made new friends on the scheme who had also been pushed aside in school but were very committed to the work they were doing, even though it was painting and not bricklaying. I know a few of them who have gone on to have successful businesses and are earning far more money than any of the teachers who told them they could not do anything with their lives.

With £29.50-plus travel expenses, it was just short what I was earning as a paperboy and window cleaner, and I had to give up, so I went to work for a large production factory.

It was true what critics claimed that the scheme enabled employers to exploit school leavers as cheap labour, and it provided little substance in the way of genuine education.

When I got a job at a factory, it was overwhelming for a sixteen-year-old. I had always worked or been around people my own age. The place was so big, you could get lost just going to the toilet. It was so bright and white that you needed sunglasses. The production lines were full of television sets and people rushed around to empty them and pass the sets on to the next part of the factory.

The company was expanding fast; it was well known in the community that if you worked there, you would be safe and there was much less chance of unemployment. The managers stood out a mile among the workers; they would often leave their desks and tell them to work faster.

Factory life was interesting with many rules and regulations, which included not being late. It was also where I would meet friends like Oz and Lee who are lifelong friends of mine today.

The pay was far better than I was earning as a paperboy and window cleaner, and my pay tripled overnight, and with overtime and living with my parents it brought a good social life.

The work itself was what was referred to as 'backbreaking labour'—at least in my case (putting parts to the back of the television set). The speed of the line was bottlenecked by the humans, not the machines. Therefore, this was adjusted to just below what was possible for a human to handle. This would make me sweat, and it felt like work.

It was a wakeup call being shouted at in front of people by the managers. Some of the managers just knew that there weren't better jobs out there for that skill level and preyed on that by telling me that if you didn't do overtime, they could get rid of you.

That said, it wasn't all bad—I put my head down and after a few run-ins with the managers was given a permanent job which gave me the platform to pass my driving test and get drunk on the weekends.

Within a year of passing my test, I was driving and not focusing on the road. I was extremely lucky, as I had put my seatbelt on just five minutes before the crash. I was driving into a dual carriageway and a car coming towards me at around fifty miles per hour went straight into the side of me when I was going slowly.

The bang stuck with me for a while afterwards, and as I got out of the car, I could see it was totally smashed and a complete right off. Most people would have gone home but after the recovery pickup lorry came and took the car to a garage I just wanted to go out with my mates on the town. The next day the shock came, and I ended up going to hospital and didn't know what was happening to me while going to work.

I had bruises and had whiplash with pains hitting my back. It shocked me to think what would have happened if I had not put my seat belt on, as I ended up smashing into a traffic sign as the car hit me off the road. It was certainly a wakeup call and up to this point I have never had an accident like that since.

It was the people working at the factory that made the job and there was always a party over the weekend, and I still don't think I have ever had a better social life than in those six years at the factory.

But being around different people brings a different cycle of friends and that was the time when I started smoking cannabis which led me to smoking and recreational drugs at parties.

In those six years it was party, party, party and that's all I thought about, starting on a Thursday, hungover on the Friday, and out straight from work to a club until Sunday some weekends. Many weekends I didn't see my parents and would come home and change and go straight back out. The one good thing about a big organization with thousands of employees was that it brought money to the town. I had seen how the valley's businesses suffered after the coal miners headed to town for work and how shops began to close.

The town was full of people on a weekend. There wasn't a bad night to be in town starting from Thursday and finishing on Sunday. Sadly, today the businesses have left the town in recent years and the place has become a ghost town with shops boarded up and pound shops everywhere. As normal, it was the working class, that would suffer with higher levels of substance abuse on show in the town now.

With more money in my pocket meant more drinking and drugs and I would end up with no money on the Monday and do shifts as a barman at our local pub to pay off my book, which was the debt I had after spending all my money.

I did everything from weekends away to trips to Ibiza and festivals tripped out on LSD. Trying every drug available apart from heroin, it seemed like a good time, but it was soon to catch up on me as it was affecting my work, and even when a manager pulled me aside and asked me if I was taking drugs I carried on.

Last going off I lost so much weight and went down to nine and a half stone and looked awful. I had given up football which I had recently returned to, and I was starting to feel paranoid. I wasn't as talkative to people, and I started to isolate myself at times and leave the club with without anyone knowing.

In my final year of working at the factory I had started a relationship with a girl who had a baby, and I took the role as stepfather on with pleasure. My family welcomed them with open arms.

The relationship only lasted around eighteen months and there was some good times, but she could be very hostile, and I didn't know any better at that time, and I took what happened to me as I would never hit a woman in my life. Even her brother witnessed me getting thrown down the stairs. I just stuck it out and hoped that it would change, but it didn't, and I wanted out of the factory and the relationship.

I was angry for some years afterwards until I met the girl in the pub one night and she said sorry. With what I know about mental health now I totally understand more than I certainly did back then, and I forgave her within a heartbeat. Sometimes you have to have a bad relationship to find out what happiness really looks like when you are in a good one.

I had been there for five years when I started to realise that I would never get anywhere as my face didn't fit. I even trained up with one of the manager's cousins thinking that I would get that role. It turned out that they offered him the role after only weeks of him being on the shop floor.

There was a lot of abuse of power, and they just wanted people who challenged the workplace to leave. There was one young lad on a twilight shift who urinated on himself because he was not allowed to leave the production line; he was so ashamed he never came back. The food court was a five-minute fast walk, and with only fifteen minutes for a break there was no chance of having a real break due to the queues waiting for the food. This was the just a few things that we had to deal with for years.

I was often taken into an office and offered my notice when there were no union representatives in the same room. My mood was always up and down, that feeling of being trapped like I had experienced in school. I failed to do anything about it. I didn't try to undertake additional education, nor did I train for a new role. Instead, I unconsciously choose to stay in my comfort zone, blaming everyone else for what was turning out to be now a miserable time in my life.

I thought of joining the army at one stage, just to get out of this place which was now making me feel low. Seeing mangers coming into work with their company cars and smiling was just a pipedream for me. I looked for other jobs, but there was nothing that would pay the same and all I now knew was working in the factories.

The final nail in the coffin for my days at the factory was when I was working on the other side of the building away from my friends. There was no radio playing music and I could not even talk to anyone near me.

The last thing that shocked me was when my grandfather on my dad's side of the family was in hospital and had only one or two days to live. Some of the family left because we didn't know how long his last moments might be, but me and my father stayed throughout the night. As I came back to the ward after going to get a coffee, my father came out crying and said my grandfather had gone. I rarely saw my father cry in front of me and we wept on each other's shoulders.

My grandfather lived to eighty-eight years of age and spend more than forty years as a coal miner. My grandmother was in a care home at the time, and it was all getting too much for the family. After no sleep all night, I went into work to explain that I would not be working that day and the reason why I could not even think of being there.

The manager looked at me and said, 'Why do you need a day off? Get on the production line, we have no one else.' I said, 'If you make me work today and I have an accident on the machine, I will make sure I sue you and the company.' Then I walked away.

I was tired mentally and physically and didn't care about the job anymore. I was still living with my parents but would rather have no money than take the verbal abuse that some of the managers were dishing out to me and many others who could not leave because of their rents and mortgages.

Standing up for myself and not being a robot for the factory managers felt better than money. I told all my mates as I left and went on the sick for as long as I could. It took me years to understand that whether you have a boss who calls people names, or there's a leader at your organization who thrives on embarrassing people who make a mistake, dysfunctional leadership can be a serious problem.

"I choose a lazy person to do a hard job. Because a lazy person will find an easy way to do it." – Bill Gates

I know now that no job is for life, but it was mentioned a lot in our family. "Settle down, get a good job and stay there for life." However, my thoughts were, why would I want to spend most of my life in something that I hated? It didn't make sense to me.

After returning from Magaluf with my friends, I decided to quit that job and sell timeshares in Tenerife. Unknown to me, the boss of the timeshares business was notorious in the criminal underworld.

Four million visit Tenerife each year. But behind the sunshine image lurks an underbelly of violence tied up with some of those involved in the expat timeshare world. Some of the employees were from all kinds of backgrounds, including armed robbery, fraud, and GBH.

However, some employees were like me and were there to earn as much money as possible in a short time and get home in a few years or even settle in the sunny climate. It was the perfect lifestyle, I thought, and I was given a five-star apartment.

After the first day's work I was told to come to the office and explain to them why I was having a party at the complex. I was twenty-one and I have never been so scared in my life as I was then, and I am not afraid to admit it as these were men I had never encountered in my life before.

I was later told that if I didn't do what they said, my kneecaps would be missing the following day. I didn't last long, just about a week in the end, and I liked the way my kneecaps looked so I headed to Los Cristianos until my flight home.

What it did give me was a taste of a new career which I didn't know at the time.

So, after I came back from Spain. I felt like I was a complete idiot, that low self-esteem that I had come to the forefront of my mind. I had no job, no education to speak of and no money, much less chance of getting my job back. I felt angry, betrayed, and let down in myself.

Unbeknown to me, my life was soon to change. After waiting in the dole queue for a soul-destroying hour, I saw a job as a sales representative on the advertisement board. I was offered the job but had to explain if I had any offences as I would be dealing with money.

I had previously been in court for a few minor offences, like urinating over a policeman when I was tapped on the shoulder thinking it was one of my friends. One time I was locked up for being drunk and disorderly, and I woke up thinking I'd painted my bedroom white when in fact I was in the police cells.

There was also a time when I was on drugs and ended up in court for affray for breaking up a fight with a man who was drunk and was hitting a woman. It was embarrassing when the court read out exactly what I said when I was drunk; it felt like they were talking about someone else.

It's not an excuse for my drug taking and drinking, but only in recent years experts have explained the root of ADHD is with

36

how dopamine is transmitted to the brain. Our brain relies on dopamine for optimal mental functioning. When this relationship is distorted, symptoms of ADHD can begin to arise.

Could this be contributing to people struggling with substance abuse?

When you look at UK prison studies, they have indicated a rate of 43 per cent in 14-year-old youths and 24 per cent in male adult's screened positive for childhood ADHD, with 14 per cent have persistent symptoms. Those with persisting symptoms accounted for eight times more aggressive incidents than other prisoners and six times more than prisoners with antisocial personality disorder.

After a face-to face interview in my home, I was given the job. I suddenly felt I was in control of my own destiny. If it was to be, it was up to me, and I had to make sure I would never have to que in the dole queue again. I dreaded it. I hated being spoken to like I was a lazy stupid scrounger by the man who was looking over his computer at me.

After now being employed again, I decided to book a holiday to Turkey. It was a week of hard drinking and partying.

Following that week, we landed by plane on a Saturday with no intention of going out when there was a knock on the door to go out with my friends. I had no intention of leaving my bedroom but after ten minutes I agreed to go out to a club in the next community.

It was that twist of fate that would change my life forever. At the club I came across a girl who I had danced with after ending my relationship with my ex-partner and never thought I would see her again.

It was too early to start a new relationship and ten months later I was in the same room as this girl. That girl was the girl I would marry and would change my road in life.

Michelle didn't even remember me dancing with her which said a lot about my sex appeal, but with my fake designer clothes and orange tan, something clicked. After chatting all night, Michelle explained that she was going on holiday with the girls. I give her my address and said, "If you want to see me again, send me a postcard".

On the last day of Michelle's holiday, the postcard arrived through the mailbox, and I was over the moon. We met up the following week and went on our first date together. Michelle was stunning and was at university. I had never known anyone who had been to university among my circle of friends.

We saw each other when she had time and when I could get over to the next valley where she lived. Her parents had moved to Bristol, and she had a flat with her friend. If there was ever a knock on the door, I was told to hide behind the sofa as it was usually the rent man.

After only a few months together while out with my work mates, three days before Christmas, another traumatic event happened. I was coming home on the bus when two of my mates told me that they were so sorry about my grandmother, but I replied back that she was fine now. There were no mobile phones back then and I headed to my home. I could tell straightaway from my mother crying that something had happened.

My mum explained that my grandmother had had a heart attack and died. I was in total shock and started punching the wall. My nan was the last person I would even tell that I was smoking, and I loved her more than life itself. I just couldn't get my head around it that one minute you were looking forward to sitting down all together as a family for Christmas and the next minute she was not here.

I just couldn't process what had happened and ran to her house with my grandfather and uncle upset. It was a sign this was real and happening and we hugged each other like I did with my parents. I was staring into space.

It changed my life again. You are here on this earth one minute and could be gone the next. That was the turning point when I realized that you must live the best life and do what you want to do as it can be so short.

After my grandmother's sudden death, I felt that I had to live for today because I didn't know what was around the corner. I wanted to experience as much as I could of the life that had been given to me. I was obsessed and I was haunted for years by the feeling that I was going to die suddenly.

The more money I earned, the more I spent. I took my wages for granted. I was flashy, buying new items; all my money went on having experiences. I remembered the teacher saying that I would do nothing with my life; on top of that, the death of my grandmother was feeding this obsession.

Over the coming months we met up and there was nothing serious, and after coming back from travelling around Europe for a month and giving up a job to do something I had aways wanted to do, something was now clicking together.

The love grew and after a year we were spending more time together than ever and I was having more fun doing the things that happy couples do in life. We booked our first holiday together with friends to Jamaica and bonded our relationship.

Working on the sales side, I was now wearing suits instead of coming home dirty from work. My mindset was changing, and I was growing in confidence. It was a sales manager who built may confidence and something that I took with me throughout my life. Fake it till you make it he told me. This is an expression in which a person imitates the confidence or skills they need to succeed in what they are doing in the hopes that they will eventually feel real. Proponents of this idea say you can fake confidence and hope that, eventually, it will inspire real confidence.

I attended conferences and heard speakers talk about motivation, and I was taken in by everything they said. I would leave thinking that I would love to do that one day.

I worked harder than ever before as I could to spend money on educational tapes and books about positive psychology. I made my car my own personal university, I was enjoying learning about things that really mattered in life.

One of the greatest theories, I learned about was the "Ericssons 10,000 Hour Rule." According to influential research by psychologist Anders Ericsson, tells how the path to expertise is available to anyone who's prepared to put in the necessary levels of practise. He also explained that his concept of deliberate practise does of course require a raw mix of motivation, good health and opportunity. He suggested at least 10,000 hours of practice spread over a period of ten years.

Having a passion for positive psychology, I was to find research uncovering tentative evidence that people's characters can be strengthened by adverse experiences, such as surviving a disaster or living with an illness.

I learned about the 80/20 rule, or Pareto principle, is a prediction model applied in a variety of business settings to determine factors that affect success and improvement. It states that, in general, 80% of results come from 20% of causes. The 80/20 rule can help you optimize your workplace productivity by guiding your analysis of tasks, time allocation and responsibility delegation.

One of my trainings talked about growth and involved the Hierarchy of need. Abraham Maslow's hierarchy of needs is one of the best-known theories of motivation. Maslow's theory states that our actions are motivated by certain physiological and psychological needs that progress from basic to complex.

Abraham Maslow first introduced the concept of a hierarchy of needs in his 1943 paper, titled "A Theory of Human Motivation," and again in his subsequent book, "Motivation and Personality." This hierarchy suggests that people are motivated to fulfil basic needs before moving on to other, more advanced needs.

The physiological needs include those that are vital to survival. Some examples of physiological needs include Food Water Breathing. At the second level of Maslow's hierarchy, the needs start to become a bit more complex. At this level, the needs for security and safety become primary.

People want control and order in their lives. Some of the basic security and safety needs include financial security, health and wellness and safety against accidents and injury.

The social needs in Maslow's hierarchy include love, acceptance, and belonging. At this level, the need for emotional relationships drives human behaviour. Some of the things that satisfy this need include Friendships, Romantic attachments, Family relationships social groups Community groups. At the very peak of Maslow's hierarchy are the self-actualization needs. Self-actualizing people are self-aware, concerned with personal growth, less concerned with the opinions of others, and interested in fulfilling their potential.

Why was this never taught at my school? Wasn't this far more important than learning about algebra, which I have never used in my life?

Working face to face and cold calling on the streets was extremely hard some days. The abuse we received, and people shouting and screaming at us and telling us to go away was something that I took to heart at first. I would tell them I was just doing a job and mostly they settled down; they were frustrated and took it out on me.

Some people spat in my face, and that was worse than being punched. I felt like the lowest of the low but just had to take it; we could not react as we were the face of the company.

It was only about five percent of the people we talked to that were horrible. People told me to get a proper job; I would tell them to find me a job where I could do less than thirty hours a week and earn between £600 and £1,000 pounds a week and I would take it.

I was now known in sales and was working my way up the ladder, gaining the respect as a great salesperson. The money I was earning was far more than the teacher was earning who'd told me I would not do anything in my life. I was able to afford the material things that I am now no longer interested in, and the company car parked outside my parents' house demonstrated my success, or so I thought at the time.

We didn't think twice of booking holidays and would just head for the sun every few months. Michelle had finished her degree in business, which at the time less than a handful had achieved in her council estate, and I was proud of how she'd achieved this at the same time as doing three jobs.

My diary was now getting full in January, and I would book anything to the point where I wasn't even enjoying the experience; it was just another tick off my list of things to do each month.

I would book a supercar experience even though I have never been interested in cars and couldn't tell you anything other than you put petrol in it and it goes from A to B. But there were things I wanted to do like adrenaline-filled sports such as bungee jumping, white-water rafting, driving a small plane and much more.

I found I was good at selling and listening to people, but when I got to the top and achieved where I wanted to be, it was the case there was only one way to go and that was down. I was at that point that I would get bored and change my company.

Sometimes I would have three jobs and still finish by four in the afternoon during the week. The time I was off I would impulsively buy stationery and things that I just didn't need.

Again, this would have a concern in our relationship as we decided to get married after I proposed on New Year's Eve Millennium, and we also wanted to buy our first house. There were other issues that would cause distress as well.

"Failure isn't fatal, but failure to change might be." – John Wooden

Chapter 4

Change

When I was not feeling good, I would say to her that I wanted us to move to Spain and leave, which was my way of saying that I could not handle the things around me, and it was, in my mind, a way to escape. I just didn't communicate back then and didn't want my troubles to affect Michelle.

I was over-thinking everything, and lying to Michelle about my emotional well-being was making her felt worse as she thought that I was not interested in her anymore, when really, I was more in love than ever.

After passing her exams, Michelle had always wanted to go to Australia and work on a working visa for a year. I had already done what I wanted to do and had woken up in a different country by travelling around Europe and meeting my mates in Greece for a week of partying.

I was now in a job where I was making so much money and was even offered a higher position in Accrington, England. I had a great manager and was left to do what I wanted to do as long as I hit my targets.

I didn't want to go, and I knew that it was make or break, and I would never and still today would never stop Michelle from doing what she wanted in life. I had to decide and after not too long I was all in on going down under. We gave up our jobs and waited for our visas with our backpacks on our shoulders headed to Gatwick Airport.

After travelling around Baila, we headed to Australia where we would aim to pick fruit to earn money. In 2000 I never had a mobile phone, and the only communication was by pay phone. Our families didn't know that we were in Australia and were just relieved that we had made contact with them.

The reason behind them being relieved was that at around the same time, there was a fire at Childers Palace Backpackers Hostel on 23 June 2000 which killed fifteen backpackers—nine women and six men.

Our families knew that seven of the victims were British, and to think we actually went past the hostel when it was burned down only days afterwards and stayed in that area. It was sad to see what had happened to people our age who just wanted to enjoy their lives, which had been taken from them in a heartbeat.

After a few months working and travelling around Australia it was off to Thailand where we met a couple on their honeymoon. One day while going to the beach, a group of young children headed out to sea. We could see that they were in trouble and all but two of the children came out.

Me and Mark went running out grabbing our bodyboards and headed out to them. We didn't think twice, and the current was strong. As we approached them one by one, we were getting tired, and the children were extremely tired as well. I didn't know how we were going to get back to shore, and I started to worry.

It was then that I had this idea to come together and the four of us to start kicking our feet together. As it happened it worked, and I couldn't believe how far out we had gone as we put our feet on the beach totally wiped out of energy.

After seeing the two children united with everyone it was just a relief, and to be honest, I don't like to think what would have happened if we hadn't got to them in time. It certainly deep down had me overthinking about what would have happened if we hadn't worked together and had drifted out to sea even more.

After talking to people about what happened we did hear that it was common that children and men had died out in the sea. I couldn't believe that there were no signs or anything to warn people and that a human life was not valued as it was in our own country back then.

The trip was one of the best things I have done in my life and with no jobs, cars and debt to pay off we had to start again. Michelle had moved in with my parents by now and within the month I had a job and Michelle went back to work in the job that she had left behind.

Slowly we started to save money again and bought a car. Nothing could ever take away the experience of travelling. Money comes and goes but life experiences stay there forever.

I was now working for a new company, and it was not the same. The manager was just horrible and didn't care.

Everything in my life outside work now was going well, but the pressure of reaching targets was sometimes having an impact on me. I would be in the gym every day and eating healthily and then I would have a run of bad weeks that would change everything.

I would eat sugary food and stop going to the gym. It was all or nothing, and I would drink more in the evenings to stop my racing heart, thinking of the next day ahead. I would drink wine and go through bottles of it each week. I have never been dependent on alcohol, but it was easier to give in rather than spend the evening thinking about it.

The lessons, I learned in sales and marketing would help me throughout my life. It never ceases to amaze me just how capable we are when we take the first step and keep going. I learned that habits can be both negative and positive. Habits creations always work the same, whether that be a good or bad habit.

A cue, internally or externally, will automatically trigger the action, either physical, mental, or emotional. Which in turn, delivers a reward. We know there is always a reward, otherwise it would be a habit. There are many research studies, that shows after a length of time of doing something once, it comes part of our lives.

Over the next few years, I would have periods of again keeping myself fit and then go back on a bender for weeks. I then needed a goal, and that goal was to run the London Marathon to give me a purpose to keep on that good path. I even gave up smoking and raised a few thousand pounds for the lifeboats.

Lifeboats is a voluntary organization that relies on donations, and after my experience in Thailand I wanted to do something for them. I had watched the race each year as a child, and I said to myself that I would do it one day. True to my word, I finished it in just over four hours.

Up to this point I had jumped jobs so many times in sales; I needed to stay in one job long enough to think about buying a house in the future, but I had this chronic boredom and restlessness. It was a feeling that I had to keep doing something all the time.

I had been in sales a long time. Although my life outside sales were perfect, I didn't have a sense of purpose. Deep down I knew that I was born to do something else with my life but didn't know what it was. I was now coming up to twenty-eight years of age and was a little lost when it came to my direction in the workplace.

If I was around people who were positive, I was alright, but working outside in the winter was hard for me. Some days were so cold, but we had to deliver the targets, or the managers were on our backs. We didn't have any mobile phones when I started in sales, but now we had them the managers would sometimes phone us every hour to find out how we were getting on.

Every day had that Monday morning at school feeling, that anxiety that you have to go back in and perform. You could have the best week ever and be the managers' favourite and the next week they would be screaming on the end of the phone.

I felt I was trapped; we had booked our wedding and was looking for a new home. I was in this circle, that I could not get out of, as were living a life that I could not just go down to minimum wage.

After moving into our new home, the year before, we were happy and planned to get married in Cyprus the year afterwards. With all the family we wanted to go, apart from my grandfather and uncle, and we had a blessing a few weeks later and at that time I was ready to be a father. It was one of the best days of my life when I got married. I remember Michelle and I taking a break from the family and sitting on a sofa sharing our dreams of becoming parents. I was excited about having a child Michelle said she was ready as well. Everything was coming together; we didn't want to leave Cyprus because it was like a fairy tale.

Having a harmonious relationship with my extended family has been a blessing. It has strengthened the bond between Michelle and me, knowing that our families support and accept our union wholeheartedly. I am grateful for the love and unity that we share, as it is not something that everyone experiences when marrying into a new family.

We started trying for a baby and, to our surprise, Michelle fell pregnant very quickly. I put it down to the amount of Guinness I was drinking at the time! We couldn't believe it when the test showed positive; we went to the cinema that night but neither of us could remember what happened in the film.

I had believed it might take longer for Michelle to become pregnant. In fact, she was already pregnant when we booked a trip by coach around the east coast of America with my family. My father gave up smoking after fifty years because he wanted to live so that he could see his grandchild grow up.

I was in totally shock that it was real and that my life was going to change forever... And forever it did for other reasons as well. After the thirteen-week scan, everything had sunk in and we decided to tell our friends. The response from my mates was, "Where are we going to go to wet the baby's head?"

I didn't know what to expect and the pregnancy was fine with Michelle, and seeing the scans of our baby gave me goosebumps. We spent all our money on everything we could to provide the best for our new baby. I had only ever heard all the great stories of being a parent and how it was going to change our lives. How little information did I have, was the best thing to happen to me. Being a father was the start of something that would change my life forever, including my career and my outlook on life altogether.

I certainly believe that not knowing I had ADHD and becoming a father had an impact in the first year of fatherhood. I was not just thinking of my own mental health, but I was also going to have to support my wife Michelle and a little human. I was expecting this to run smoothly, cut the baby's cord, and end up playing happy families.

Fathers became a regular fixture in the birthing room in the 1970s and today 96% of men attend the births of their children and yet there was no real information om what to do if something went wrong and certainly no talk that new fathers may be affected for a wide range of reasons. In 2004 I did not know anything about depression, let alone postnatal depression. We had gone to all the antenatal classes and were excited about becoming new parents. Never once during these classes was it brought up about the things that may not go to plan.

Over the weeks we met other couples who were just as excited as us, and we were shown everything other than a conversation about the struggles that come with being parents for the first time, of which we had no idea at all, and had only ever heard all the good things.

The only conversation I had about fathers being in the labour ward was how many had fainted, and that was talked about as if it was a joke. I found this to be just as funny and did not understand the logic behind the reason why some fathers could not cope being with their partners.

We talked about the benefits of breastfeeding and how breast was best. We also talked about care for the mother and how to support mothers better with breastfeeding. All the talk was about the mother, and rightly so, but there was nothing about how fathers can be impacted during what we know as the perinatal period.

Nobody told Michelle that sometimes breastfeeding is difficult and, like most fathers in the classes, I just felt like a spare part.

The perinatal period is during the antenatal and postnatal period, which is such an important time for the parents and the development of the child. I had not read any books on fatherhood as I didn't know they existed in 2004. I just thought that I would go into the labour ward, have a bit of gas and air, cut the baby's cord and leave as one big happy family.

Leading up to the time, the twenty-week scan with the photos in our pockets was a wonderful feeling and was on the last end of what we expected to be life-changing. I could not believe that our first child was going to be a boy. I was already planning things in my mind and the things we would do together for the rest of our lives.

I was so excited to tell my parents and in return they were just as excited, as they were going to have a grandson. We had both worked so hard in our jobs and put ourselves in the position of not having to worry about money. Like most fathers at this time, I was expected to return to work after two weeks and start earning following all the expenditure on doing up the room and the getting the best for our baby.

I was starting to think that maternity services were there just for mothers, and I was okay with that at the time as I just wanted Michelle to be safe and have the right care needed to bring our new child into the world.

The weeks after the scan went slowly and I wanted the time to come fast. I put in as many hours as I could to give us extra money. It was the end of November and the time to become parents. The pregnancy had gone well up to this point and we were more excited than nervous about the delivery. After all, there was nothing to be concerned about as there was no talk of anything going wrong.

It was a Thursday evening, and we knew it was time to go to the hospital. However, Michelle decided to watch an episode of the soaps before getting ready. As we picked up the ready-packed bag, we headed to the hospital, which was only five minutes by the car from our house.

As we entered the maternity suite, we were shown to the room which was to be occupied by the three of us, including my mother-in-law. As the midwife examined Michelle, we were told that Michelle was not ready to give birth and would be examined again within the next hour. That hour turned into another hour and then a few hours until the early hours. At this point Michelle had been up all day and was getting so tired. I was starting to think that this wasn't even mentioned in the antenatal classes. I just didn't think that it would be this long, and I started to get a little anxious.

My best friend and his wife had just lost a baby while Michelle was pregnant, and I could not believe it had happened to such caring, wonderful friends. I started to over-think that things were not going to plan for us. As always, Michelle was so calm; she even told me it would be okay as her eyes started to close.

Around 6 a.m. we were in a different room. The midwife asked Michelle if it was okay for a student midwife be present and help. It was time for Michelle to be induced to bring on the labour. After the midwives left the room, I reached over for the gas and air to have a go at breathing it in, as many of my friends had said that they had done the same.

When the midwives came back into the room, they reached over to the wall to turn on the hospital radio. Suddenly this came on loudly. Both midwives looked at each other and could not believe what had happened. We all laughed, thinking that someone was looking over us, which was comforting.

In the next few minutes, the midwives went out of the room. Suddenly three doctors came into the room and explained that Michelle needed a C-section and was to go to the theatre. I didn't know what this was, and I started to panic.

I was having a panic attack in front of everyone; I had never had one before. I felt so guilty as now all the attention was on me and not Michelle. I was given a bag to breathe into. As I settled, I was now extremely worried and had not been prepared for this, and I didn't know what to think. My mind was racing, and I couldn't believe that this was happening.

I was told by the doctors that they needed to take Michelle down to the theatre and to get ready if I wanted to be by her side. Soon I was gowned-up and was told to wait outside the theatre until I was called in.

I opened the door and went in to see Michelle. I just could not believe what I saw, as I brushed past all the knives that were placed on the table. As I saw Michelle's face, and she was so worried, I held her hand. I was in total shock and silently prayed that everything would go well.

All I was waiting for was the baby to cry, which didn't happen as expected. I didn't know what was happening and then as I looked over to see our baby on a table with the doctors over him, he started to cry out loud to the relief of both of us.

As I went over, the midwife handed over our baby and said it was the boy we had been expecting. I was then told that I was to take him down to be weighed. I was so worried about my track record of dropping things, as I had never ever held a baby so small in my life.

I must have walked slowly down the corridor, as it felt like slow motion. I took him back to Michelle and held him close to her chest. It was all over. We had a son and decided to call him Ethan by his middle name Thomas, after my grandfathers.

I was expecting the three of us to go home and start family life. That was not the case and, after running into town to get a present, it was time to go home on my own. As I entered my house and put the key through the door, the house was so quiet. I decided to knock on my neighbour's door and invite myself in for a drink. I just could not believe what had just happened and felt emotions that I had not experienced before. I didn't know what to think; it certainly wasn't this overwhelming feeling of love that I was expecting as I was just relieved that they were both alive and well. I felt what I know now as anxiety and that night I did not get the sleep that I wanted. I jumped in the car and headed to the hospital, looking forward to seeing the both of them.

As I walked into the ward, a midwife was standing over Michelle talking. It was like Michelle was in a daze, and she looked confused. I walked up to Michelle and the first words she said were, "I'm so glad you are here, Mark." I could tell straight away that there was something wrong.

I had no insight that Michelle was unwell; I'd just put it down to her being tired. Michelle explained that she had no sleep as there were mothers snoring on the ward. I looked at my son who was sleeping and gave her a hug and told her it would be alright.

It was not alright, and Michelle didn't want me to leave. I didn't want to go as I helped bathe Ethan. He was so small and started to cry for the first time of my visit. I could see in Michelle's eyes that she was not right, but I did not know what it could be and again put it down to her being tired.

After people started to visit, there was small talk from Michelle and no excitement in her voice. It was strange and even though I didn't get the feeling of love that I was expecting after having a baby, I just didn't investigate it. It was only later in Ethan's life that I understood the difference.

After three days we left the ward and headed home. The house for some reason seemed so quiet, the banners on the walls, balloons and cards filling the room. It was December and I had already put the tree up as we knew there would be little chance of doing it when the baby was to come along.

After a few hours, there was a knock on the door from friends and family coming to see the baby. For me, it was so overwhelming, and I didn't have time to think. It was great to have people share their joy with us, but for us we just wanted to have time alone with Ethan.

I couldn't get things ready and always had a problem with time. I must be on time do the things that are necessary, and this always caused tensions as Michelle is always late. What I know now is that so many people suffer from time anxiety, and with a baby it can take forever to get out of the house.

After a few days Michelle still could not sleep, and she looked unwell. I was home helping with the baby and didn't have a clue, so it was good that the family were there to help. Michelle had set her mind that she was not going to breastfeed, and I was there to support her decision.

Michelle felt that she was glad to leave the hospital, as she felt in a way pressured into breastfeeding. The house was a complete mess with presents scattered all over the floor in our small living room and baby clothes everywhere.

For me, the whole routine changed and the feeling of not having Michelle bounce off with conversation was not good for my own mental health. Michelle sadly said that she wanted to go up to my parents as she felt uneasy. She didn't seem right at all, and I started to worry if she was okay. I didn't know any of the signs to look out for; and after all, we didn't have any conversations in the antenatal classes about it.

We packed a bag, and I phoned the health visitor to say that we would be at a different address and headed a few miles up the road. As we sat with my mother, Michelle looked lost, and it was as if she was talking through my mother. I had never seen this ever before and didn't know what to think.

As the health visitor came, she wanted to be alone with her and asked us to leave the room. I was now thinking that was this because of me and I had done something wrong. After about fifteen minutes the health visitor called up the stairs and asked me to come down with them.

It was the first time I heard the words, "I think Michelle has postnatal depression." I looked stunned and asked what that meant. I didn't have a clue; I had never known anyone in my family to be open anyway about suffering with their mental health. We sat down with a coffee together and worked out a plan for the next steps.

Knowing Michelle was now getting support was a relief and the health visitor was just an angel. The way she talked to Michelle and reassured her that admitting she needed the help was the first step in her recovery. The health visitor did not talk over Michelle, she just listened and showed empathy and understanding that it happens to many mothers.

The health visitor told me that it was pretty common, and that postnatal depression affects between ten and fifteen in every one hundred women having a baby. If it was that common, it wasn't mentioned ever to me. If it had been, maybe I could have seen the signs. I was just glad that Michelle had opened about her mental health as I don't know what may have happened.

The health visitor started making some calls and in a space of ten minutes had sorted out a few people to engage with us. It was her tone and voice I remember more than anything; it was so sweet, and she spoke quietly with reassurance.

One of the first things I was thinking was that she was phoning social services to have Ethan taken off us. I know now that was not the case, but these were the conversations I wished I had known about.

I decided that I needed more time off from work as the time to return to work was approaching. My boss was amazing and as I was self-employed it was not even a problem, and he understood the situation. My boss was the first person I talked about Michelle's postnatal depression, and he understood more than I thought. He told me, for the first time, that his son with whom he was living was suffering from depression after leaving the army.

It was a conversation I did not expect. It was the first time I understood power talking. Once they have a clear understanding about mental health, it opens up a completely new conversation.

Seeing someone you love to go through depression was extremely hard. At that point we only told a few family members. I did not know how to have this conversation with anyone.

As Christmas was approaching, I cannot remember a thing about our first Christmas together with Ethan. It seemed to come and go quickly. With the new year coming in we looked at the year as we had to stick together.

Like many parents I was not getting a good night's sleep. On the top of the worries around Michelle, I always felt that I had insufficient sleep, particularly if there was a single thing on my mind. This was far bigger than I had ever experienced. We know now that a high percentage of depressed people show symptoms of insomnia and many people with depression also suffer from excessive daytime sleepiness and hypersomnia, which means that they are sleeping too much.

My mind was racing, racing and racing more and more, and I was unable to stop it and just didn't know how to stop, even if I could. I had lost interest in going to the gym and started eating terrible food just for comfort. I had this feeling life wasn't going to get better for us as Ethan was now three months old. With no income coming in I had the urge to buy more things than ever and now started using our credit cards. I had not planned for everything that was now happening as I was expected to go back to work after two weeks.

The pressure was on, and the strain started to show in me, and I started to get more flustered. I kept forgetting things and was not focusing on tasks ahead. I was not lazy; I was mentally tired and felt I could sleep all the time.

I had never spent so much time in the house. When we did go out, we wanted to go to places where no one would know us, so that we did not have to explain ourselves. We would jump in the car and mainly walk along the Gower pathway with ice cream in our hands, watching the waves crash against the pier. It seemed like heaven.

At the time, I did not know any difference in my feelings toward Ethan. Initially I had these silly thoughts that he had made my wife unwell, but of course, it had nothing to do with him. As the weeks went by, I started to enjoy my time more with him. Not having to return to work helped me bond with Ethan. I would love playing with his feet and putting them onto my chest. We now know it's so important; it releases oxytocin which is good for the father's mental health and the baby. It shoots shots of dopamine in the brain, and there are even now scans that show the benefits.

I don't know if I would have had those feelings of love so quickly if I hadn't been helping him. I could tell the difference from what I was like in those good few weeks to where I was with him now. I was beginning to appreciate the joys that came with fatherhood.

I feel that there should be more paid leave for fathers and partners, as without that time off together maybe it would have taken far longer to bond. Who knows. I had friends who had to go back to work after just two weeks and were back and forth to the hospital as the baby was on the neonatal ward.

Chapter 5

Looking for the light

I had always made careless mistakes and they occurred when I was changing the nappy. I put it inside out or upside down only for Ethan to pee all over me, which was not good when you're tired and it's three in the morning.

It was a frustrating time with hospital appointments and medication changes which all took their toll. I wanted everything to happen today. There were no real services around, only a great Community Mental Health Nurse who went on to set up the first perinatal mental health service in our local town, following her support of Michelle.

There were many reasons why I was now starting to feel depressed during the postnatal period. I would tell Michelle, "Let's go shopping and put it on the credit cards" to make her feel better, but no amount of spending money was going help during these dark times.

I had never had thoughts of suicide up to that point and I'd always loved life. But this thought was getting worse. I started to think of ways that I could do it and that maybe I just wouldn't wake up from this nightmare. At no point had I made a plan; it was these thoughts which I could not control that were coming into mind faster than ever.

I had always wanted to live and have the best life that I could. I started to think about losing my grandmother, seven years before. She would have known the answers and would have showered Ethan with love, as she always wanted to be a great-grandmother.

I could not tell Michelle how I was feeling as I didn't want it to impact on her mental health anymore, so I just suppressed all these feelings which turned into anger. It resulted in me hitting the sofa and breaking my hand. I was now in a sling and that caused it to be even harder while changing Ethan's nappies. I just didn't know where to turn; I just wanted to hide away and wake up when it was all over. If I'd known it was going to last a long time, I could have managed it much better. The days seemed to run into each other, and I did not know if it was going to last years. There were some good days when Michelle was feeling better, very few and you start thinking that this is it. Then—bang, it would be twice as bad that following day.

I felt totally alone, when I had family and friends to talk to about how I was suffering, but I didn't want to take the attention away from Michelle like I had when I had a panic attack in the labour ward. With my mind always racing anyway, I was overthinking the worst and thought that Michelle did not want to be with me anymore.

Previously I had not really taken much notice of the bills, as we had a joint account and Michelle was much better at it than me. It was overwhelming having to deal with so much in a short space of time. My brain was all over the place and when I did manage to get back to work, as I was self-employed at this time, I was not the same person. I could not take the pressures as before and I often ended up running away to a pub and casino until the early hours.

Of course, this came across that I was out of order, but I needed to have a break from being in this pressure cooker, and I was finding it hard to motivate myself each day even though I had this wonderful bundle of joy in front of me. When my mates did manage to go out with me, they just did not know me anymore. One night I got so drunk and shouted at my mate after he said something that previously I would have laughed off. After leaving the club, the doorman knew I was very drunk and tried to throw me out. As I got to the door, I turned around and just wanted to continue the fight.

I wanted someone to hit me to take away the pain I was feeling in my mind. I felt like I was starting to feel a burden now on everyone and, even though I was supporting Michelle, I didn't know how to support myself. Before we became parents I only had to look after the two of us. I was wondering if I was the only new father who had these feelings.

57

I had talked to people, and they said it would be best days of your life—yeah right—and how parenting is a piece of cake—yeah right to that one as well. I started thinking I was not good enough and low self-esteem started to come back in my life. I hated that feeling of crippling insecurity and inability to work. Michelle was using a mood chart, in a diary form, which is something I used, and I learned things from Michelle that I had never been taught in school about our mental health.

I was struggling with maintaining daily routines of new life as a parent with everything else that was going on in my life. It had always been a struggle, a struggle that caused me extreme stress and anxiety, so in the year that didn't go to the plan as we wanted, we decided to move home and start making better memories, which was the worst thing we could have done looking back on that time. It made matters so much worse.

One day I went to Cardiff to sort out a few things away from my town. I remember walking across the road by Cardiff Castle and thinking that if a bus hit me now that it would be all over. I felt really anxious and was now starting to scare myself. I didn't how to react to that and just went back to the car and headed home.

One day coming home after doing some food shopping, I had a phone call from Michelle. She told me that she had taken some tablets. I could not believe it and I started to bang the seats. I pulled over to the side of the road. I cannot even remember if I phoned the ambulance or a member of my family, as when I arrived home the ambulance was parked outside the house. I started to cry, thinking that I was going to lose Michelle again, and I followed the ambulance to the hospital, which was forty minutes away. This was strange, as our local hospital was only five minutes down the road.

It was seeing Michelle in the bed of the hospital that I was just about going to drop. I had to be the strong one; everyone had told me in the past and at this point I had nothing to give. I remember coming home alone and putting Ethan in his cot. And then I was weeping. Out of nowhere, huge tears, shoulders shaking, sobbing like I hadn't sobbed in years—maybe ever. I sank to my knees in the middle of my bedroom, alone thinking how this had happened. And as I wept, it sank in, for the first time, that I was not in control of my emotions. I realized that I had been suppressing my emotions for far too long, and it had finally caught up with me. It was a wake-up call, reminding me of the importance of acknowledging and should have addressed my feelings.

Michelle just could not deal with the pain in her head anymore; she couldn't see any light at the end of the tunnel. Michelle was discharged after a few days and the team came to see how she was managing. I felt that I could not leave the house, just in case something happened again.

I became extremely anxious if she was not in my sight. It was tough and lonely; it was like we were in a bubble, and we were even thinking at one point to sell the house and get a caravan in Cornwall for some reason.

With my mother-in-law now living in our small two-bedroom house, I found it hard. It was once just for the two of us, and now there were four and there was nowhere to run. My mother-in-law was an angel and Michelle wanted her, I do not know what we would have done without her, as Michelle just wanted her mum who had taken time off her job in Bristol. It was my mother- in-law saw me breakdown one day and told me to get the help.

I didn't know she was there as I was holding my hands in despair, rocking back and fore on the new rocking chair we had brought. She saw the tears streaming down my face and the look of hopelessness in my eyes. Sensing my struggle, she urged me to seek assistance, emphasizing the importance of reaching out for support during difficult times.

As the months went on and with the right medication, Michelle started to get better. Despite her being unwell, Michelle was an amazing mum and still is to Ethan. Michelle has never been the one for anyone to feel sorry for her; she just did not know how to fix it.

The house was not the same after that; there were good memories, but now there were bad ones filling the house. We needed a bigger house, but we did not want a bigger mortgage. We decided that we just wanted to be back near our families and sold the house. Moving house was one of the biggest stresses in my life.

We moved home, with the backend looking over the farm. It did not make it any better as we had even more stress from the owners who wanted us out of our old house before we moved into our new one, or the deal would be off. We were also being pressurized by the estate agent. I was more worried that it would make Michelle unwell again.

With nowhere to go, and all the furniture to move from the house, we moved our contents to my parents' house, where we stayed until the move was completed. It was the best move we made, back to the community where I always felt welcome. It was a completely fresh start. It was like a new start of my own life, and I realized I wanted to leave sales altogether. I just could not take the pressure from the job where I had become unwell.

It just showed how a bigger problem, this is in the workplace. I still feel and it would benefit companies, before employees make that change, I was lost, looking for something that would take me away and something I could do that had more purpose in my life.

At this time my mind was still all over the place and did not know what it looked like and had no goal-setting strategies in place. I started looking through all my books that had helped me in sales, but I did not know how I could transfer the skills that I had learned into another profession.

I just knew that there was something different in my life, but I could not put my finger on it and what my life would now look like in the future. The one thing I knew was that after going through with what Michelle had gone through, I wanted to be with her more than ever now the darkness of her depression was lifting.

Maybe things might have been different if someone had sat down with us both and told us that with support many parents go on to have other children and nothing happens again, but we had no aftercare for this situation.

We took the decision not to have any more children and I went to the hospital for the vasectomy. I wanted to do it as, at that point, I could not think of anything worse than having another child and putting Michelle at greater risk. I have always been happy with the one best present in life as many never have that opportunity.

Ethan was a big part in Michelle's recovery, and he also kept me sane. He was now bigger, which was easier for me as I found it hard holding a little baby having thoughts that I would drop him, but now he was everywhere, climbing the sofas and exploring the world.

It is funny how fatherhood changes you for the better and how it improved my life and purpose. Everything I wanted to do in the future was for him. I wanted him to be proud of his father, like I was of my own, working in the mines and being the supportive dad.

I learned to take away some of the beliefs that my father had from his own father. My grandfather was a wonderful man who had the old beliefs that food should be on the table when he got home and was glad that I didn't take that one.

Life in our new home was better, and being around our family even more was so much easier with my father now coming up to retirement. He was always there if we needed to go anywhere. My mother just loved also being a grandparent and I could see the delight that it brought her having Ethan.

Ethan brought so much meaning to our family and you could see how happy my parents were and the love they showed him.

"If you're not prepared to be wrong, you'll never come up with anything original." – Sir Ken Robinson

I needed a new purpose in my life and realized that money did not matter to me anymore. All the material things that we buy in life come and go and your health and happiness should be top of your priorities.

I phoned the local volunteer centre and was put in touch for an interview. I found a role volunteering with young people helping to prevent them from going to prison. The role was perfect, and I started doing my training, which was free to attend.

At this stage Ethan was only eleven months old and with support from parents and Michelle now back at work it was an opportunity to give something back for an hour a week. It was the start of a new career, and I grabbed the role with both hands. I felt that I was now doing something that helped me as a child, and if I helped one person that was good enough for me.

The role was with a charity, in a mentoring scheme which involved mentoring a young lad who just needed some guidance as he was not doing well in school. He had got into some trouble and his mother was worried about him. He had no father figure in his life and no family around him apart from his siblings. I was able to introduce him to experiences he hadn't had before; one of these was the gym, and he loved it.

I spent a few months with him until it was time for me to move to someone else who had what I now know is ADHD. We got on well; he was just as lost as I had been in school about what to do next. I showed him how to play snooker at a club, and he seemed to enjoy the sport.

My role was all about listening and finding out what these young people wanted to do, then seeing if we could make it happen. I took the time when other people said that he was not capable and enrolled him into training as a carpenter because he loved woodwork. He had no intention of learning the subjects like French and Geography that were being taught to him, but he was good with his hands. School was just a waste of time to him, but now he had a purpose and that helped him make a different circle of friends.

I was looking for more permanent paid role in this area that would support my family. I had no intention of going back to sales, but I really missed the money. I spent some time as a security guard looking after lorries at night and took a job as a postman, but due to the early mornings and putting the letters in the wrong post boxes, I didn't last long.

I knew that there was something around the corner and if I stayed out of sales, I would find something I enjoyed. I wanted that feeling that I was doing some good; coming home feeling proud of myself was priceless.

After a while, I decided to go back to my youth club that helped me as child. It was local and just done the road from my house. It was there, I would meet up with Stan "the man" again. As soon, I walked into the club, he gives me the biggest smile. I explained that I would love to volunteer and from that moment he granted me the space to create anything that I would benefit the young people.

Sadly, in our community, there would be worldwide press with The Bridgend suicide incidents, where at least 26 young people committed suicide in Bridgend County Borough in South Wales in 2007 and 2008.

Reports speculated that a "suicide cult" was to blame, though police found no evidence to link the cases together. The national press was a disgrace, and we were offered mental health and suicide prevention training. It was at that point that I started to think what I wanted to do for the rest of my life. We learned about why we shouldn't use the word "Commit Suicide" and replace it by died by suicide in the United Kingdom.

We had to remember that suicide is defined as the act of intentionally ending one's own life. Before the Suicide Act 1961, it was a crime; and anyone who attempted and survived suicide could be prosecuted and imprisoned; also, the families of those who died could potentially be prosecuted. In part, that criminalisation reflected religious and moral objections to suicide because of the belief that it was self-murder.

It was lazy journalists affecting everyone, let alone the family members who had lost their loved ones. It was not just the town; it was our community.

In 2010 police asked the media to stop covering the suicides to prevent copycat suicides. Bridgend is a former market town of around 39,000 people; however, the suicides stretched over the whole county borough of Bridgend, which has a population of over 130,000.

I wanted to work in mental health but didn't know how I could get started with no experience. It was also important to have lived experience as well as the right training. After all, my working experience was only working in factories and sales with no formal qualifications.

I was now applying for jobs outside of sales and took a huge pay cut and soon had a temporary job in a cake factory. I even paid for HGV lessons, and I was terrible at driving them. In the same year a few days before we were due to fly to Egypt something changed overnight.

I was to see my own father go through a psychotic episode when he had a high fever, lack of calcium and lack of sleep. He thought he was seeing bugs in the room. At the crisis point, he was just wearing a vest in winter and tried to jump out of the window because he thought my mother was part of the IRA. He was picked up by the police and was so worried about him.

It was scary in the hospital where he was treated. He hugged me tight, pleased that I was still alive, but he talking to someone in the corner of the room. Forty years ago, maybe that treatment that lasted a few days would never had happed and could have been locked up in a psychiatric hospital. My father's own experience made him fully aware that it can happen to anyone. I often say to people that anyone can have psychosis at any time of their lives.

What my father's experience did was bring us closer together. Today we had those conversations about mental health, and he was fully aware of how anyone can suffer. My father already had compassion and empathy for people who could suffer after seeing Michelle go through her dark days. I felt that this experience certainly changed him for the better.

I missed an opportunity to talk about what I had gone through and didn't want to tell him that his son had suicidal thoughts and had suffered in silence. At that time, my mental health had improved, and I didn't think it was the right time to bring it up. What I know now is that anytime is good time to have those conversations around our mental health.

On the job front, it was by a lucky chance that I saw an advert about an open day and just walked into the room and asked for an interview. I talked to every single person there and was laughing and joking to everyone I was around. I think they loved the way I came across and offered me a job.

I was on my way in my career and wanted it more than ever after my own father's experience. I soon found a job working with people who had learning disabilities and mental health illnesses.

The job was perfect again though with very low pay, but it was a great start. I was soon offered lots of training and was building my confidence. I loved the role of supportive living, and it helped change people's lives. I wanted to do floating support work to learn from other projects and that is what I did for a whole year.

I didn't have any help with my career pathway. I didn't want to work as a carer in a nursing home, which often came up at the job centre; I wanted to be a support worker, which is an entirely different role.

The hours weren't good: I had to work in the morning, come home and then work from 4am to 10pm. I was missing Ethan and Michelle at the peak times of their day, but it was over four days, so I made the most of our time together when I was not working.

The role of dads in the UK has changed beyond all recognition in the past 50 years. Today, fathers no longer want to be limited to the role of family breadwinner and disciplinarian; they want to be true co-parents, providing nurture and be with Ethan.

The project had about six people living there. We could take them out in the van to the cinema and we even had a food allowance for a meal afterwards. I was getting paid and was out on my own with no managers around to tell me what to do. I was enjoying the new experience.

The residents had cerebral palsy, and some had a no verbal communication. There was one lady who had been cared for after her mother died – she was a real character. Another lady was a lot younger and had learning difficulties; she suffered from bipolar as well. I was myself around them; we had a great laugh and made it fun. Seeing our household income cut by hundreds of pounds each week was made easier by the rewards of helping people.

Sadly, I was going to encounter a stressful time; while working, one of the support workers was mentally abusing vulnerable people without me in sight and sometimes in front of me as well. The person had been there a long time, and I could not believe what I was witnessing. I felt exposed to something that I had never encountered in my life.

After discussing my concern with two other new staff members who also had witnessed the same, I had to speak out and went straight to the manager. To my shock nothing was taken seriously, and I wanted to offload to the senior. The senior was great and took it to the head of the office above the manager and the motion was in place to safeguard the most vulnerable people in society.

The police called me in to make a statement and were taking the case very seriously. The case went to Cardiff Crown Court, and I was told I would have to give evidence. The two female members of staff were scared, and I reassured them that, with support from the organization, we would be alright together. That support never came from the company, and instead the support came from each other. What I saw will stay with me forever, but I have since processed it.

The day before the court case started, the person pleaded guilty and would never work in this field again. However, he only received a suspended prison sentence and was given community service. I was just relieved that he would never be working around people who needed that support again.

The following week, one of the parents broke down to me and thanked me for protecting their son and asked me if it was sexual abuse. I explained that it wasn't and the relief that came from his mother who wanted to just protect her son as any good mother would do for her child was palpable.

Looking back, whistleblowing can be a "battle of conscience". "Only the truth will set you free," I don't care if people are late or maybe sometimes lazy, but this is life and death. "If I find myself in a situation where my conscience tells me that speaking out is the right thing to do, I will do it." After my experience, we must always update and reform whistleblowing laws. "The law needs to be more user-friendly, more accessible and less judicial."

"I have no regrets about the action I took," and still today "I feel proud to know I was strong enough to stand up for what I believed in and didn't know that it wasn't the last time I would be put in that situation to safeguard people that I cared for and myself as well.

With no support from the company and the manager who did nothing and was still in the role, I felt something was wrong and disheartened. I was just needed something for me, and it was at that point I returned to martial arts, which I hadn't done since I was a teenager. My uncle would take me to the local dojo (gym) and I had loved the competition.

The one thing I always remembered was 'Leave your ego at the door'. It is a common phrase that I have seen written on the walls of martial arts gyms where I have come across many people who have the biggest egos but nothing to back them up.

I started to look further afield and started a job in criminology, which I was interested in. It was Michelle who found the perfect job for me and got the job. I started to work with patients from Broadmoor, Ashworth and other high-risk patients who seemed lower risk now.

A forensic mental health facility was a hospital that provides mental health services to people who have been accused or convicted of a crime. The purpose of a forensic mental health facility is to provide treatment to people with mental illness who are involved in the criminal justice system.

I was interested in all the training that was provided again and learned more on the job. I was working with nurses who had so much experience and were always asking questions. My mindset shifted and like a chess player I had to learn to be one step ahead of what the patient was thinking.

I was also learning so much from the patients about the time they had spent in these hospitals. Two patients with whom I had a good repour with had spent forty-four years in Broadmoor and the other twenty-two years at the same hospital.

Overnight I was thrown into protecting staff and myself while giving the support that was needed to the patients. In the two years I worked there I saw the most horrific things that no one would understand unless you had worked in the same field yourself.

From self-harm to the extreme, alarms going off sometimes three of four times when someone was trying to end their lives, to psychosis when people thought they were Jesus or had been abducted by aliens. Many staff members were attacked, and restraining patients was the norm on every shift. It was high pressure and mistakes could cost lives. Over twenty people had started when I started the role and only two were left in the space of two years and the other person was admin.

The high staff turnover was a problem, but the management didn't have a solution. If the shifts were covered, they were happy, yet many staff were off work because of their mental health and that was impacting on services. It was also affecting their confidence, and that brought unemployment and struggles to their families.

I was sometimes attacked. Due to the company not looking after its staff, my life was sometimes in danger. Also, we had some agency staff who just wanted the money for a shift and did not listen to important handover information.

One time I told an agency worker to look after a lady all the time as she was on five-minute observations. As luck would have it, I went past her room while the support worker was reading a book. The lady had climbed under the bed sheets and was trying to take her own life. If we had not raised the alarms, that lady would have died in a matter of seconds.

There was a box which was like a black money box, that was where the knife was kept safely to cut people down from trying to take their lives in the nursing station. As soon as the alarm would go off, someone would run to the box and open it up by a key and to get the knife out then run to the patient. It was like a race for time and every second counted. Only recently when I went shopping in a store, I seen something very similar, and it brought back that memory.

The stress and pressure were now starting to get to me and was on my way to burn out. It was a factor in one of the worst things that I did was during a night when a patient. The patient had been granted leave to help him back into the community and was alright leaving the unit. This patient had spent time in prison; we would find out years later that he had lied thinking he would have an easier time in our hospital, but his stay turned out to be far longer than his sentence.

I had always had a great rapport with this patient; we talked about weight training and fitness. When he came back after a whole day on leave, we knew that if he was out of control and was on drugs, so our plan told us we had to go into the nursing station and phone the police.

As we searched him when he returned to the ward, he became angry and started to shout and scream. It was clear that he had taken something while on leave; this was not the person I was used to. As I tried to calm him down, he said, 'I am going to rape your wife when I get out.'

In a moment of madness and impulse, I started going towards him and said something – I can't even remember what. I couldn't keep my anger inside. I had never behaved so badly before, and I was endangering other staff members. He could have killed me and hurt the people around me.

I was told to calm down, take a break then to go on a different ward. The next day I owned up to everything; I had been out of order and was ready to give in my notice. My manager said that the patient had apologized for his actions, and he didn't want me to get into trouble. I couldn't believe it and left my feelings what was said in the office and within the hour was back where we had been lucky for me.

New starters who wanted to have experience as trainee psychologists and had witnessed the same as me became affected and left. Fear is an emotional response induced by a perceived threat that causes a change in brain and organ function, as well as in behaviour and the patients could sense it. One patient, just looked across the room at one new starter and shouted out "here's breakfast".

It was not for anyone, and some were left traumatized and unwell after not having the support from the company.

I was working with rapists, paedophiles and sometimes murders who had done the most horrific tortures to their victims. I was just getting desensitized, having worked to many hours was less likely to feel shocked or distress at scenes of cruelty or suffering by the overexposure.

After being on a shift with twelve patients and a nurse I knew it was time to move on as the company was more concerned about money than safety and care. I know that people in the private sector are still getting compassion fatigue and are burned out due to the lack of support and putting themselves and others at risk. This should be a criminal offence and more needs to be done by inspectors.

"Failures are finger posts on the road to achievement." – C.S. Lewis

Just wanted to play, my mum holding me tightly and my father (Far Right)

Should be ADHD not ACDC on t-shirt.

With my trainer, Billy.

Happy Days - Our wedding day.

The start of a hard time.

Four month later I was in community mental health teams.

Dad takes call for mother and baby unit to minister

Campaigning to reopen the mother and baby unit in Wales.
It opened seven years later.

The online abuse was hard, talking about postnatal
depression in dads.

Good Morning Britain, talking about birth trauma and PTSD.

Fathers with perinatal mental health problems are 47 times more likely to be rated as a suicide risk than at any other time in their lives (Quevedo et al, 2010)

76% OF UK
SUICIDES ARE MALE

510,000

What is the biggest killer in men under forty-five? Why are new fathers not even asked about their mental health.

Articles hitting the front page.

My youth work, helping the next generation.

Coaching my boys football team. We learned so much from losing many times.

My Ted Talk about fathers' mental health.

Waterstones, launch of my first book.

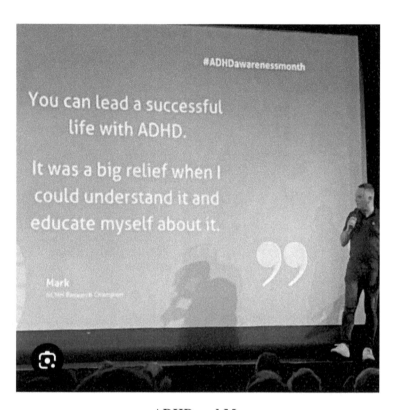

ADHD and Me

With my supportive MP Chris Elmore, outside Westminster with my report on why dads matter.

My friend and Mentor Dr Jane Hanley.

My first Love

Chapter 6

False Hope

In the same year everything changed for me once again. As a family we were caring for my grandfather at his home who had dementia, and my uncle gave up his job to care for him full time. Watching someone you love with dementia just fall away from his true self each day was horrible. It was also hard for my uncle; living with my grandfather was all-consuming. It required a lot of his time, dedication, and patience. It was also hard on my mother to see someone you love in that condition and to neglect your own health and personal life to provide the care that was needed.

The support outside was not available, only again by the charities that were filling the gap, which should have been there by the government. The lack of government support for caregiving was evident, leaving the burden on individuals and charitable organizations. This not only highlighted the need for better social policies but also placed additional strain on families already struggling to cope with their loved ones' conditions.

When I would take my turn on a Sunday to give my uncle a break, in only those few hours I found it upsetting trying to put my grandfather on the toilet and wash his own behind. Even through the hard times, we found humour together. There was no way we wanted to put my grandfather in a care home, while at least it was impossible to keep him safe, which was the highest priority for us as a family.

This man who had been in my life had worked hard in the mines and just wanted the simple things; nothing more than that was dealt this hand in life. At times, through tears, I could see how guilty my mother and uncle felt, though frustration, at trying their hardest to care for my grandfather through dementia.

I loved my grandfather so much and when he died it had an impact on me. I saw him take his final breath like my other family members. He simply lived his best life. He smoked a pipe, did a few pounds each week on the horses which he studied. He worked hard in the mines and was a quiet man who liked a pint on the weekend socially. He lived with his family and dog and that was important to him.

We know that people often experience depression or anxiety after the death of someone close. We don't usually think about them having posttraumatic stress disorder (PTSD), but it can also happen, especially after a catastrophic death.

Within weeks my mother phoned me while in work with the news I would never think I would hear, she had cancer. I remember bouncing against the wall, in the town centre and couldn't grasp the words clearly. She wanted to tell more as soon as she knew and never once shared to me that she was getting unwell.

I knew that she was short of breath at times and was looking pale, but there was no way I was thinking she would have cancer.

She is clear of cancer today but at that moment everything that I had put at the back of my head came to the forefront altogether at once. I just couldn't think and was totally numb with everything which I had experienced during the postnatal period as well.

This time it was becoming worse. I was becoming very unwell with suicidal thoughts in my mind. I was paranoid and had physical symptoms. I was pretending to go to work and would sleep in the car in the woods as I didn't want Michelle to find out. I was again masking my feelings and was telling everyone I was alright, but inside I was dying.

It was making me the biggest liar ever; I would say that I was okay when I needed help. I didn't want to end my career and have anything on my notes that might affect my work, but the pressure to provide for my family hit me like a ton of bricks once again.

I didn't know how I would get the support that I needed. My mind was playing tricks, and my anxiety was beginning to overwhelm me.

87

You know how you feel when you leave the iron on in the house or think that you left the door open? You can't think straight until you have checked. Now imagine you believe that there are seven irons on in each room and seven doors unlocked. How would you feel? The answer is: totally overwhelmed. You can't think straight.

I didn't know where to start. Thoughts of how I was going to do it were starting to enter my mind. I had everything to live for, but I didn't want to wake up with this numb and horrible feeling every day. It was stressful on my body, and I wasn't looking after myself. I was eating and drinking more than I had done and I just could not cope. It was like all these demons that would normally come out from under the bed one at a time were coming out at the same time. I felt that I was going mad.

This went on for many months and every day was the same. I went from the odd day to waking up having this dreaded feeling and wishing I was still asleep. Through these months, depression went underground. Feelings were dangerous. There were too many dark and horrible thoughts going through my mind to tell anyone. So, I kept emotion under wraps, even more so than in childhood of the anxiety I had suffered. Nothing phased me outside the house and even at home I showed almost no sign of reaction to anything, even while churning with fear and anguish.

I missed many happy days, felt shame as if I were faking, and obsessed over every one of my failings. Depression pushed into every corner of my existence, and both work and family life became more and more difficult. Having just won a national kickboxing tournament for my age range, I was physically in the best shape ever. Four months after winning that event I was in a car one day heading to work and broke down in the car park.

I was shaking, rocking back and forth, banging the dashboard and then just crying and crying and crying. It was a total build-up of everything that I had never dealt with professionally. It was a relief that it had happened as I was so paranoid thinking that everyone around me would be better off without me in their lives.

The turning point was after an hour in the car when I thought, I don't give a fuck about anything, but I had to be here for Ethan. If Michelle left me and lost everything, as long as I was alive to see him grow up that was enough. I phoned up for help and the recovery was underway in community mental health teams.

Why had I done this before? It was the shame, and I was mindreading every situation. It was also because I was brought up in society that it was a sign of weakness and that we should be the man was some of the barriers from speaking out and addressing my needs that could have killed me.

"If you don't try at anything, you can't fail... it takes back bone to lead the life you want" – Richard Yate

I was put on medication that helped me to focus on the therapy I was offered, and I embraced everything that was needed to live my life again. I had a great counsellor. After accepting and admitting my fear, I tried to chase negative thoughts from my mind to picture what it would be like to win this battle with a big smile on my face.

It has come to my attention in adulthood that the "approval of my parents" has served as a stumbling block not just for me but for my family, friends, and so many others that I have encountered over time.

Of course, this isn't anyone's fault, necessarily—this is how our parents were raised and their parents before them. There has always been a very definite cultural understanding of "living the dream" or "success," and each generation builds on the previous generation's successes and failures to create expectations for the generation to follow.

I had talked about my failures and not making my parents proud in my own head. The reality was that my parents had always been proud of me and didn't want achievements to be the focus point. My parents didn't have to tell me that "I love you" really every day, as I knew it, but something I have learned is that I tell Ethan every day, and he gives it back.

I was having sand tray therapy, a form of expressive therapy, is suitable for people of any age and can be used to explore imaginary worlds. It can be particularly helpful for grief or trauma when verbal therapies are stifled. Cognitive behavioural therapy (CBT), based on the idea that our thoughts about situations can affect our feelings and behaviour, can also be helpful. For example, overthinking about someone's reaction can lead to negative emotions and unhappiness. Sand tray therapy and CBT can help individuals overcome stifled verbal therapies and access innate creativity.

I've learned to keep in mind, though, that other people's responses don't necessarily reflect on me. Seeing that everyone has unique challenges and life events has made it easier for me to turn my attention from self-doubt to empathy. I've been able to engage with people in more peaceful and joyful ways by adopting this mentality.

I had no idea there were so many kinds of meditations to choose from when it came to mindfulness. Mindful munching involves focusing on the flavour, texture, and aroma of the food you're consuming. Another type of meditation is a body scan, where you focus on each part of your body and observe any sensations or tension. This practice can help you become more aware of your physical state and promote relaxation.

Mindful Mandala Colouring: Filling in intricate patterns with colors while focusing on the present moment.

Mindful Body Talk: Engaging in positive self-talk and affirmations while being aware of your body and its sensations.

Body Scan Meditation: Lying down and systematically scanning your body from head to toe, paying attention to each part and any sensations you may feel.

Sitting Meditation: Sitting comfortably with your back straight, feet flat on the floor, and hands in your lap, while focusing on your breath or a chosen object.

I had worked hard, and it was not easy as everyone would be fine. I was building my confidence again, which was one of the first things to go with my depression. If I had one problem in life now, I only had that to deal with not all the other things that I had buried in the back of my mind.

It was now back in the gym and eating healthily once again. I always from then on told Michelle if I was having a bad day and that made it easier. Michelle understood depression just as much as anyone else. Being a father again was enjoyable as it always had been, but it had affected me during those dark moments.

It was at the gym that my road in life would change for the better again.

I asked a gentleman if he had finished with the weights and said he had to take his wife to National Health Services (NHS) Prams as she had postnatal depression. I said my wife had postnatal depression as well. In that moment we talked side by side while doing our workout and I told him things that I had not even told my counsellor.

Brian had lost his home, his business, and had become unwell himself. It was Brian, who sadly passed away while I wrote this book, who was the inspiration to start Fathers Reaching Out. He became a very good friend who had issues with alcohol and drugs for many years until he found God and was at this point a pastor at a local church a few miles away.

I went to the building where other professionals and services were at and set up Fathers Reaching Out, surrounding myself with them. It was Michelle's idea for the name, and she supported me all the way and still does today.

I had let my mental health get so bad and I wished I had opened earlier to Michelle, as by this point, she had become unwell after looking after me and had changed her job, herself working for a mental health charity where she is still happy today.

One thing I needed to focus on was the way employers treated mothers, and of course fathers, in the workplace. The way my wife was treated was disgraceful at a big blue-chip company. Michelle had never taken a day off in the twelve years at the company and was then told "Can you do the job anymore?"

To hear that Michelle was asked about suicide and things that the managers did not have a clue about and the fact that they'd let her go in the state she was in was criminal. It was not long after that Michelle was back in the crisis team and was unwell once again. I was so glad that she left the company months later and found her purpose working for a mental health charity, and now also works as a youth worker.

"Everything you want is on the other side of fear." – Jack Canfield.

Fathers Reaching Out was created to support fathers whose partners had postnatal depression, but it developed more than that after fathers were suffering themselves. Other groups were running at the centre. There were groups for anxiety, veterans, mum's groups and many more which was easier to signpost and follow them. The father's group was working well, and we were learning on the job how to reflect and how we could do even better.

I met fathers who had lost their babies. I met fathers with babies near death on neo-natal wards who weren't even asked how they were coping, and that impacted on the relationship and the development of the baby.

Some fathers were so depressed that they couldn't even provide the basic needs for their baby, and it looked from the outside that they didn't care. They were so unwell that, like me, they used negative coping skills to manage. It was an eye opener when fathers opened up to me and told me that they couldn't see their children and babies because they couldn't disclose how they felt.

Before becoming parents, many fathers had a history of anxiety and other disorders that were risk factors. They had thoughts of harming their babies but would just disappear down the pub and couldn't tell their partners. One dad I became friendly with a father who had psychosis and thought the baby's head was the devil.

The plan was only to set up one group in my local town of Bridgend, so I advertised it in our local gazette newspaper. I wanted to make sure that everyone in the Bridgend County was aware of the service we were providing. What turned into just a advert, went further than ever expected.

They wanted to know why I had set up the group to run a story and explained how it affected me and other fathers I was now supporting. That one local story went national and suddenly, I was asked to go on radio for BBC Women's Hour.

I wasn't expecting what was going to happen next and it just went BOOOMMMM. Within weeks I was on BBC Breakfast, national radio stations, and I was asked to attend meetings which of course caused me to develop imposter syndrome. I was experiencing so much engagement on social media from around the world; 60 per cent of people were positive and detailed how they felt as fathers, but the other 40 per cent were scared and hurtful. The comments were "Man up", "You didn't give birth",

"Just another cope out", and I was now, outside of my circle of friends, exposed to people that were of course having issues themselves.

I needed to carry on for the parents and thought no one was in the car that day when I needed help and was around the people who really mattered, which were my true family and friends. I said like I did when I got the help "Fuck It" and carried on the fight.

What I know about life it can change for the better and worse within minutes. This time it was Ethan; He had been acting differently and wasn't himself. We had kept him off school and our gut feeling as parents knew something was not right. That day we decided to take him to the hospital as his temperature was getting worse.

We sat in the emergency department and, after an hour, were told to come in. I explained to the doctor that something was not right, and after checking with him, he explained that it was just a temperature and that I should give Ethan some flu medicine. Me and Michelle were worried and thought it was much worse. As the evening approached, he started to look at the floor and was totally spaced out. His eyes were not normal, as if he were seeing things.

Within hours, we took him back to the emergency department at the hospital, and we wanted to see the doctor again. As we went in, our local doctor was there, Doctor Mohammad, who had known us for many years. After seeing how worried we were, he started to check Ethan out, and within two minutes, he said that he needed to go to the children's ward.

The fear in his voice of concern changed how we felt, and we were now anxious about not knowing what was going to happen next. The doctor assured us that it would be alright and that he was in the best place. Seeing my son on the bed having a test, all things were coming to mind. The thought of losing him again, like I had experienced in the labour room, came to the forefront of my mind.

After tests we were told that it was pneumonia, I didn't know what that meant for Ethan. We were told by the nurses, that it was the best thing we did was to bring him to the hospital and that it may have got worse. Ethan was now getting the right treatment and was in good care. As the days passed, he was enjoying the attention but had lost so much weight in that time.

I couldn't believe that the doctor had just discharged him and that he had not picked up on it. I was just so thankful and still thankful to my local doctor Dr Mohammad who knew us and Ethan family history. It is rare to have a regular doctor today like I had Dr Richards growing up who knew everything about our family. I thinks it's something we have lost in services if I am being totally honest.

Every time I see Dr Mohammad, I always bring up that night and how thankful we were for taking us seriously. Many people associate pneumonia with the elderly, but it is actually the biggest infectious killer of children worldwide stated by UNICEF. I dread to think what could have happened if we didn't use our gut feeling as parents.

Within months I was invited to the Maternal Mental Health Alliance, and I was there when it started. The Alliance has been responsible for mothers to have better services in the United Kingdom, and the work they have done so far has been life-changing for thousands per year.

I was even awarded Inspirational Father of the at the Welsh Government buildings. Taking my mother and father for a free lunch and seeing people making a fuss over me, I could tell they were so proud. My father, who would not normally go to such an event, picked up the courage and was there to see me on stage.

It was that my father is not a social person, he would talk to anyone. But he finds it had that people he doesn't know; don't know he is eighty percent deaf from the mines. The communication can be difficult for anyone with so much damage to his ears. Crazy to think that my father had five hundred pounds compensation and cost him two thousand pounds years later for hearing aids that didn't work for him.

Six months later myself and Michelle, went to Grosvenor House in London to pick up my local hero award at the Pride of Britain awards. Walking down the red carpet with Michelle was an experience. We drank the finest champagne which was left on another table and going to waste. I talked to so many celebrities, but the real inspirational people were the ones who had done amazing things in society.

As the event was getting ready for the after-dinner party with a Radio One presenter, I waited for Michelle in the corner of the bar. There I started speaking with a lady who was dressed down compared to use all of us in suits. After five minutes Michelle came back, and the lady asked if we would like to meet someone we knew.

As we went into the back room and unlocked the door, Professor Stephen Hawking was in front of me. I just could not believe it. I had never been star struck before apart from the time I met George Best, but this was unreal.

As I sat beside him, I asked if we could have a photo, which he agreed to. It was that moment I marvelled at how within twelve months I had been so unwell, and now I was in recovery to sitting next to this great man...

After going back to our five-star hotel, the last to leave along with a member from Westlife, it was back to reality and work. It was the same year I met Dr Jane Hanley. I was lucky to have a meeting with Jane, who would become my mentor at a pub near the university where she was working. Jane had written a book called Perinatal Mental Health for professionals.

I had a good understanding of mental health, but this was out of my depth. I needed more knowledge in order to prevent the patients from acting out their thoughts, so that the fathers would avoid situations where they could even cause harm.

Some fathers had been victims of sexual abuse and had not discussed their experiences until their mood state reached crisis point and they felt the urge to be more protective towards their new baby.

Jane explained paternal mental health, and it was the first time I had heard those words, and also "perinatal mental health". Jane told me that the clinical signs and symptoms of paternal depression are like those of depressed mothers.

To work with Jane, it was an honour and quickly trained me up to even start working with her own her own training. Jane had worked so hard to get where she had got to and was one of first people to push the agenda on perinatal mental health. Over time,

Jane would become a good friend and loyal to me which I found rare outside my own circles of friends growing up.

They would include low mood and a lack of enjoyment in life. However, when fathers are depressed, they tend to bury their emotions sometimes by using alcohol, drugs, avoiding the family home and of course struggling to bond with their babies.

Everything that Jane was telling me had happened to me and the other parents I was now talking to, and they felt safe to really open about their feelings as they knew I had been there too.

Jane and I just clicked and over the years we have written countless articles on front covers for the Nursing Times and other journals. We have written two academic books together for professionals, delivered training together for hundreds of health visitors and midwives, and most importantly become good friends. I was honoured to work with someone who had been discussing perinatal mental health for forty years and was a pioneer in the field.

I took note, that someone who should have been at the top table, when discussing this area was pushed aside, even people who she had helped along the way didn't want to get her involved anymore and it was all about them. Years later I would find it laughable, that there were all these roles in perinatal mental health and not one for a role about fathers.

It was why we had to do it ourselves and start a business to survive and do what we loved. We have never been businesspeople; we are just two people that care and have passion for change. I will even bet my own house, that you will never find two people that are as passionate and caring for parents to have the right support. But I knew that things happen for a reason and all I could do was keep going.

"I have not failed. I've just found 10,000 ways that won't work." – Thomas A. Edison

At the end of that year, I was invited to deliver my first ever talk. It was in Rochdale for the charity Mind. They had never heard of a father's postnatal depression story before and also shared with naming names as an advocate for all the fathers I had supported and who had offloaded their lives to me.

Again, I was now invited to ITV's Good Morning Britain and was involved in campaigning for change to support every parent in their mental health. My week was full; I was working in the hospitals and delivering talks voluntarily. I was also very much involved in my local youth club that my son was now attending.

The charity was getting bigger, and I didn't want to go too fast as I was aware of getting the right people to run them and all the policies that come with that need. I was working all hours and had fathers who had planned to take their lives and I had to break confidentiality many times.

One day I could be at the Mind Media Awards around celebrities and on television shows like BBC Two's Victoria Derbyshire, Sky News and Radio Five, and the next I would be cleaning the toilets at my youth club. It wasn't just the once; I was asked to return when a story around fatherhood would be on their agenda.

Despite the lack of sleep and financial constraints, I was determined to make a difference in the field of mental health. The adrenaline and passion for my cause fuelled me to give my best during each appearance, knowing that even a small impact could have far-reaching effects.

I believed that my sacrifices were worth it, as I wanted to make a difference in people's lives. The thought of potentially saving someone from the pain and struggles I had experienced motivated me to push through the challenges and continue advocating for mental health awareness and that included sleeping in my car many nights to save money on hotel costs.

I was always up for new challenges, and I hoped I could help even further in my quest. I had seen some of my friends end up in prison, and some were fathers to young children. Witnessing their experiences inspired me to explore the prison system where I could make a positive impact on both individuals and society.

One of the biggest prisons in the country was only a short journey away, and I was asked to speak there at a writing festival. The day was run by a wonderful man named Phil, who gave me a chance to speak with the inmates. The talent in the room was incredible. Some had written poetry and showed their stories about their tattoos, and that opened them up about their feelings.

There were some amazing speakers who had been in the prison system. One of them, like me, grew up in the East End of London and after a lifetime of crime turned his life around. He was now involved in numerous projects in television and had become a published author.

There was another ex-inmate who grew up in an environment of crime and found himself going down the same path as his father, who had also been in prison. He decided to take control of his life and get support and is now a bestselling author.

It was so inspiring that these men could help to give other inmates a different outlook in life by sharing their stories. Again, post-traumatic growth was staring me in the face.

There were people who had served twenty-odd years in prison and were now consultants. One ex-inmate, who had left prison with only £47 in his pocket that and was later proved to be innocent, now works for BBC Panorama and on many other projects.

Seeing these men share their stories showed that investment should be about prevention in the first place rather than using people who had been there and worn the T-shirt to warn the next generation. I feel that is the key to success in stopping more people end up in a life of crime.

It was a pleasure to be asked back and speak to dads who had been locked up away from their families. It was heart breaking to see how they talked about their children and made voice recordings for them at bedtime.

Some of the dads had just made one mistake in their lives but lost everything in that moment. The guilt they experienced and how they hadn't seen their children on the outside for many years, made me think about how I would cope if I couldn't see my son.

I could be finishing a twelve-hour shift in the hospital and then coaching the football team to jump in the car to Manchester media city to be there for live television in the morning and back again after a few hours' sleep.

That is something I would never recommend as even though at the time I was preaching about looking after yourself and lowering your stress levels, it took its toll on many occasions. I just thought if I didn't do it who would and the help that and understand it may cause.

I was now hyper focusing on all the research, and everything I was saying at conferences was backed-up by references that were out there, but there weren't many at that time.

My paid work was as an Independent Mental Health Advocate (IMHA) and I was trained in the Mental Health Act 1983, and I supported people in understanding their rights under the Act and to participate in decisions about their care and treatment. I was working with one or two high profile offenders and the next I would be working with a mum who had paranoid schizophrenia and was unwell.

I was not employed by the NHS or any private healthcare provider and was there to provide free, independent, and confidential support. I learned so much from that role in the next two years and loved it, but the office staff apart from a few were toxic and jealous of the good work I was doing and saw me as a threat. I didn't care about going up in the company; all I cared about was looking after the people who needed the help.

It was happening again. I couldn't be around certain people. I would feel like I was being manipulated into something I didn't want to do. I was always totally confused by their behaviour, as if I was defending myself to this sort of person. I continually felt bad about myself in their presence.

I needed something else to focus on and joined the boxing gym to fight in a three-round bout. The ADHD was the driver, once again and needed a different purpose outside my working and family life after winning a national kickboxing championship and quit afterwards.

I took all my frustration out in the gym and sparring to let off steam. My boxing didn't last long after getting knocked down in the fight, but it kept me away from thinking of the situation I was in as I didn't want to worry Michelle.

After taking my son to a football match and becoming violently sick in front of him because of the toxic office environment, I didn't want to waste anymore of my energy around these people. I had to look after my own mental health and was telling people to do the same, but I wasn't myself, so I changed my role to become an agency worker.

I worked for six months in a housing project trying to house people who had been made homeless. There was little housing available, and it was horrible seeing families made homeless. It made me realise that many people are only one wage packet away from being put out on the streets.

Some of nicest people who walked through the door felt shame and guilt that their children had had to pack a bag and leave, and all their toys had been put in storage. I had people who were moved to different areas and didn't have any family around them for support with their mental health.

I had to do all the assessments for their mental and physical health. I had to ask them what medication they were on so that it could be delivered. We were not rushed and could take as long as we needed to make sure people felt that they were being listened to.

It was heart breaking, when I knew that I would be going home to put my feet up and watch television and they would be in some horrible hostel surrounded by people who had problems with substance abuse and trying to keep the family together.

How did parents cope with all that noise and banging going on in the hostels around their children? I had a lot of information about mental health that the other members didn't, and I learned fast on the job.

I was then offered other projects by the agency. I loved every day, which was different for me and felt I was my own boss. The work was flexible and involved supporting people who were homeless, managing people's use of heroin and substance abuse, to people who had been victims of sexual assault themselves. The files I was reading were shocking as they had been when I first started in my career.

The jobs I was referred meant I had to have a lot of empathy. Many people in helping professions—such as nurses, therapists, social workers, and first responders—show up to work with big hearts, ready to help others. But the reality is supporting people through their traumatic situations can be a trauma of its own, called "secondary trauma". It's especially common among helping professionals. The chronic stress of taking in others' trauma can lead to symptoms similar to post-traumatic stress disorder (PTSD) such as emotional exhaustion or hypervigilance.

That can lead to Compassion fatigue which involves emotional and physical exhaustion that can affect people who have been exposed to other people's traumas or stressors. It is characterized by a decreased ability to empathize, feelings of helplessness, and burnout due to the demands of supporting those who are suffering.

"You can never know how many lives you've touched, so just know it's far more than you think. Even the tiniest acts of love, kindness, and compassion can have a massive ripple effect. You have made the world a better place, even if it doesn't seem like it." ~Lori Deschene

It was during this time I was still under metal health teams and remained diagnosed with anxiety and depression. I had been waiting to see a psychiatrist as the waiting list was long in our area.

I was given an appointment to see Dr Davies and was told that it would be at least two and half hours and that I could take Michelle. As I waited in the hallway, Michelle was sitting quietly but I was my normal self, pacing up and down looking at the notice boards.

Doctor Davies came out a few times walking past me, and I just waited for him to call me into his office. As I sat down, I was told that I would have to start at the beginning, and I was fine with that. I had told Michelle things that I had never told her before, so I didn't have to hide anymore about things happened before we met.

As we started talking, the doctor asked me questions. The doctor just listened as he took notes down and looked up when something shocking was said. I told him about the substance abuse, the feeling I was having each day that I'd also had in school and outside of school.

We even talked about all the silly things that I did from leaving the water tap in a hotel and flooding it, to being the first to jump in trolleys to be pushed down the road, unaware of the danger. I'd had near-death experiences that could have gone wrong when I was drunk, as well as everything that I have told you about in this book.

101

Then after offloading every detail with the help of Michelle, I was asked a series of questions, not even knowing what they were for. My mother also shared her version by letter and explained what I was like growing up.

I also explained that I would become very anxious when Michelle was late, and that the biggest disagreements we had in our relationship were in the car. Dr Davies explained that was "time anxiety", which I had never heard of before in my work but was apparently quite common.

I had read something about Parkinson's Law which is the old adage that work expands to fill the time allotted for its completion. The term was first coined by Cyril Northcote Parkinson in a humorous essay he wrote for "The Economist" in 1955.

He shares the story of a woman whose only task in a day is to send a postcard – a task which would take a busy person approximately three minutes. But the woman spends an hour finding the card, another half hour looking for her glasses, 90 minutes writing the card, 20 minutes deciding whether or not to take an umbrella along on her walk to the mailbox … and on and on until her day is filled. But never heard of time anxiety ever.

Then it came out after nearly three hours: "Mr Williams, you have ADHD." In total shock, I asked, "What? ADHD? I thought only children have ADHD." He said, "No, Mr Williams. You have had it all your life and will always have it, though it may become more manageable as you get older."

I looked out of the window, and I could see that the rain was disappearing. I wanted to find out more. I asked him a series of questions including why it had not ever been picked up before. He explained that there was not much research in adults, but now more and more people of my age were getting the right answers.

He also explained about other issues that could make my life easier, like a dyslexia test. He said that that we could go down the medication route and have me talk to other people who had just been diagnosed. Dr Davies said that he would offer another appointment, but it was not for six weeks which was fine. After all, it had taken nearly forty years to get the answers. What's a few weeks? I was grateful.

He then said that "I am retiring after thirty years, and I will not be able to see you for your next journey." I wished him the best and thanked him as we went our separate ways.

Michelle would say to me, "Go down the shop and buy a pint of milk," and I would come back with everything but the milk and spend the hour talking to someone I had just met in the shop. I knew all my life that there was something just not right and it seemed like an invisible enemy that I could not see to fight.

That invisible enemy was now out in the open. I always now say to people that think a diagnosis is only a label if you don't understand what it is all about and was great my wife understood. When I was diagnosed with Asthma, in my thirties after giving up smoking, I got medication (pump) educated about it to prevent and learn about it. So, what is the difference with mental health?

I found myself at a start of a regular emotional rollercoaster ride. It was a range of emotions, that I had never experienced once again.

The six weeks was hell. I was happy, sad, and feeling anger that my life could have been far easier if I had known this from the start. I knew all my life that something was just not right, and this confirmed my doubts.

I started to go to an adult ADHD group, and I met the most wonderful lady who would become a friend, called Zoe. Zoe had also been diagnosed late in life after her son was diagnosed and set up a support group in the local town.

When we met it was so funny, we could not get a word in edgeways and I explained what had happened and that I was still in denial. "Mark," she said, "Trust me, you will understand it better and you will see other people like you too."

I went to every group and spoke over the phone and met up in person. Zoe was incredible and the time came when I was to look at medication.

This time it was a ten-minute meeting with a new doctor. I was wearing my football hoodie and joggers and looked like I had just come out of the gym. He asked me, "Do you know what bipolar is, Mr Williams?" I started to get excited, telling him all about the disorder and that I knew certain people who work in that field.

I became very hyper and then I just stopped as he told me, "You have bipolar." I said that if he looked at the notes, he would find that I was getting diagnosed with ADHD. He then replied that he felt it was the wrong diagnosis.

I had just gone through this process of trying to accept what I had all my life and my whole world was turned upside down again. I couldn't believe what he was telling me within ten minutes.

He explained about the medication I would need to take for the new disorder, and I agreed. I then asked if I could have a second opinion. Could I see someone higher in position? I was then booked in for an appointment in eight weeks' time.

The eight weeks affected me at work, and I was upset knowing that I was now in the hands of the professionals who may not give me the right answers that I had been able to get from Dr Davies.

I didn't go to anymore ADHD groups and thanked Zoe for her time without explaining what the doctor had said to me. It was a long, long eight weeks which I counted down, and I finally met another doctor who again asked me if I knew about bipolar, to which he had the same reaction.

Again, I told him to look at Dr Davies's notes from the time I had spent with him and Michelle, which included feedback from my own mother. I explained that I didn't want to seek medication and walked out of the door.

After six months I was invited to speak with professionals in North Wales when I was on form explaining about parental mental health. During our lunch break a lady asked me, "Mark, do you have ADHD?" I replied, "How do you know that?" She explained that she had worked with children and adults with ADHD for the last twenty years.

I then shared my story about what had happened to me, and she told me that I needed to go back and keep fighting. I came out after my training and phoned Zoe straight away. I must have been on the phone for thirty minutes and afterward Zoe said to me, "Listen Mark, you have ADHD, and you know that now don't you."

I knew that I had to go through the process again and Zoe supported me all the way. She said that if I didn't get the right answers I may have to pay, but she knew the professors at Cardiff University who could help. Zoe came into the meeting and was educating the doctors and told them to ring the right people in this field.

It was then I was called in and finally, just after my fortieth birthday, I was given the right answers in a meeting with an ASD nurse called Pam, who was one of the best people I have ever met in explaining everything to me. Everything I was thinking all my life she had an answer for in return.

Pam explained, in any one day we all have many thoughts which automatically enter our minds and provide us with a running commentary. This is normally far higher with people with ADHD, and louder compared to people without the disorder.

I learned, there's more than one way of thinking about things. It is the way you think and what you believe to be true. It rarely occurred to me that our thoughts about events might be illogical, unreasonable, or even just unhelpful.

Everything, Pam was telling me I totally understood. It was the way, she explained that it was harder for me to process things and challenging for people with ADHD, as the thoughts were coming in far more than other people.

Pam also explained about a dual diagnosis, also referred to as a co-occurring disorder, is when a person is diagnosed with a mental health disorder and other disorders. So, I may have had ADHD and Bipolar, but it was clear for me that the biggest issue that affected everything after speaking with specialists was the ADHD.

It just taught me a lesson that mental health is a complex one that is experienced differently from one person to the next, with varying degrees of difficulty and distress. I was now learning more about ADHD and realized that it was why I had always supported people in a person-centred approach.

"Every adversity, every failure, every heartache carries with it the seed of an equal or greater benefit." – Napoleon Hill

Chapter 7

Seeing the light

It was also a great help when she introduced me to Tom, a rugby player who had been struggling himself. This young man was diagnosed with ADHD and autism. We met over the coming months, and I found whenever I was in the room with him, what I know now as a tic would become worse. Tom explained to me what had happened to him and the tics, which were nowhere near as bad as his at all. It was refreshing and, with the support of others, and Michelle now educating herself on the disorder, our relationship once again became stronger.

After three years, I was understanding the invisible enemy that had been hanging around me all my life and it was time once again to put in the hard work to manage it better. It is important to note that the exact cause of ADHD is still not fully understood and can vary from person to person. While some professionals suggest a potential link between trauma and ADHD, it is crucial to consider that ADHD can also have genetic and neurological factors. Therefore, it is necessary to approach the topic with an open mind and continue researching to gain a comprehensive understanding of this complex condition.

I soon realized, why it was important to have the right diagnosis, as the complications if untreated for a prolonged period, may lead to more for me:

- Poor work performance
- Unemployment
- Trouble with the law
- Alcohol or other substance abuse
- Frequent car accidents or other accidents
- Poor physical and mental health
- Poor self-image
- Suicide attempts

It was now four years after I had set up the charity, and after going out for dinner to get some headspace with my wife, I received a phone call from someone thanking me for my help. I knew there was something wrong and started to talk more away from the crowd.

After a few minutes I just knew that he was in a hotel room on his own ready to take his life. He wouldn't tell me where he was, and I talked to him further. I remember that he had gone to this one hotel when he wanted to get away from all his family, it was then I quickly phoned the police.

It was at that point I knew I had to do more, and that would mean tackling the policy makers and government even more than ever. I was also pleased to know that the father who had planned to take his life who was drinking in his room was now safe. It was a few years later that we would again at a football game. It also made me realise that with no funding and was overworking something just had to give in my life.

He is now in a new relationship and having access to his child. He had suffered from postnatal depression and was never asked once about his mental health, and it made me think about how many fathers there were who had died by suicide, who were never diagnosed with depression during the perinatal period.

After supporting the fathers and mothers I had on my list, I then passed the charity to another one which was national and funded. It was now time to really push for change on a more national level. It turned out to go international the following year.

I had been a youth worker for over ten years by now and had been coaching my son's football team for many years. I was having so much enjoyment, and even more seeing him doing well in sport and school. I had been very protective of him when teachers had been negatived towards him.

I was so proud when Ethan became a national champion himself was part of the team that came second in the six- a-side football tournament. And to be the coach and able to see him develop myself made me the happiest father in the world.

I never saw it coming when I was invited to do a film with Denise Welsh, who is a famous actress, and I was even invited to her charity ball in Manchester where I met some amazing people.

It was a Bollywood event and I ended up singing on the tables and getting the crowd going for what turned out to be a memorable night.

I just loved meeting and experiencing these new things. I could have just focused on making money to buy the next big house or car, and that would have taken me away from what I was enjoying the most—the simple pleasures of life. But instead, I chose to embrace new experiences and broaden my horizons. It has brought me so much fulfilment and happiness that no material possession could ever provide.

None of this means that material goods are unimportant or that they can't be a source of satisfaction. And of course, people can be selfish or competitive about their experiences. But what I feel that if more people put experiences before possessions, if more preferred doing rather than having, we would have less clutter, less stress, and a happier society."

Speaking at the House of Commons and Westminster was an honour, and members of parliament were talking about my work as well. I was now invited to more and more conferences now as a keynote speaker all over the United Kingdom.

"The only real mistake is the one from which we learn nothing." – Henry Ford

To think I was told that I would never do anything in my life by my teachers, and I was now teaching people and speaking at universities. I took a trip to Australia, New Zealand, America, and Canada delivering talks about the importance of fathers' mental health.

Some of the experiences I was now having were things that money could not buy. It was unreal the people I was meeting, from professors to doctors around the world. I was meeting with people who had been in the underworld of crime and people who had awful experiences in life and used their experiences to help other people.

My bank balance may have been small, but my life was as rich as ever. I was in a circle of incredible people, that would be growing stronger through their own experience. People I would never have met in my lifetime otherwise. I was learning from them, and that knowledge grew daily.

My life was totally different when I was brought back to earth. I had been supporting a friend who was living with his mum, a lovely person struggling with alcohol. I had lost so many friends to drink and drugs at such young ages and it always got me in the stomach. To see this young man a few years younger with so much to give if he was to recover hit me again. Lee died on the morning of the New Year, and when I carried his coffin through the church, I felt that I had failed him. I felt that I could have done more and that affected me for some time.

After speaking about it with people, I realized I was the only person, along with his family, who was there for him, and I tried my hardest to get him into rehab but there was no funding for him. I had lost so many people over the years through suicide that I have wondered why they didn't talk to me, it hurt me each time, but I had to focus on the people that I had supported and that you can only try your best. I had to think of the people you have saved.

My talks now included being diagnosed with ADHD and more information about the disorder. It is funny when they say I have an attention difference when in fact I can hyperfocus more than just about anyone when I am interested in what I want to learn. I didn't know half as much as I do today, but I remember this doctor at a general practitioners' conference where I was a keynote speaker. He asked me in front of everyone, 'Do you think you have oppositional defiant disorder, ODD?' I had never heard of it before, but I said in response that it was a good question.

I quickly came of the stage and went on the internet. Certainly, all the symptoms were there for me:

• frequent temper tantrums when people are not taking me seriously and it's a life-or-death situation

• excessive arguing with adults, which mostly happened in school. When I felt people are not following good practice, I will fight to make sure nothing is ignored.

• never obeying adults' requests and questioning rules. I question everything because many rules have never been updated. Take school: why are we still telling children to sit for hours on end and listen when they can be more creative by working together?

• attempting to annoy adults or upset people which I can say there is no harm from me to that person and sometimes people can annoy me when I know that I can be right from the patients or parents that have taken the time to disclose information to me as I have taken the time to listen.

• easily being provoked to anger/annoyance. I know I am hypersensitive in certain situations and find it hard to communicate that, particularly to my superiors who don't expect to be questioned. I don't know everything, and I would rather something question me if they feel they can add something better to the conversation.

• frequent anger/irritation. For me, this builds up and doesn't happen until there is a pattern when someone is making me feel small. When it comes to spiteful attitude and revenge seeking that what that person may

I was never diagnosed with ODD, which is defined as 'a recurrent pattern of negativistic, defiant, disobedient, and hostile behaviour towards authority figures. Making a misdiagnosis can be harmful and frustrating for everyone involved because the treatment for ODD and ADHD are very different.

However, the symptoms do connect with my behaviour though I have challenged myself by thinking that maybe it's the people around us that are wrong. If I listened to people who I disagree with and listened to that they were right all the policies that are in place now would never have happened.

There were many people out there that call themselves campaigners and never put their head above the parapet. They often agree with what people in authority say because they are afraid disagreeing with them which may affect their careers. I have never cared about my career; all I cared about was whether the services should be in place and that was the main reason why I started doing this work.

The following year just flew. I was invited to meet the royal family on World mental Health Day and talk about mental health with Michelle. The royal trio, Prince William, Princess Kate, and Harry started the day at event for their Heads Together campaign, which was raising awareness of mental wellbeing, at the capital's County Hall.

They took to the stage to speak about providing support for those with mental health challenges, explaining that together we will break the stigma forever and save lives. Then it was time to have a private chat with Prince William which just flew as I wanted to share as much information to him as possible. I don't think I came up for air and with my think Welsh accent I think it would have been better to have an interpreter.

The engagements continued with a visit to the London Eye on Monday afternoon, which was lit up purple in support of the campaign's efforts to end the stigma surrounding mental health. It was the start of something that I had never seen before, and whatever people may think of the royal family that day, it was the beginning of something different in the United Kingdom when it came to having these conversations.

I was to meet Kate at other events which involved perinatal mental health and the importance of the early years of the child's life. I could see more charities now being founded and people talking about mental health like never before.

Sadly, that brought in people who thought they could earn lots of money out of it, and good luck to them if they are doing it for the right reasons. It was everywhere, on the radio and television, so many people coming out sharing their struggles and getting rid of the stigma that has been there since the Egyptians' time.

I was also now a consultant for charities and working with people from Tommy Tippee, the NHS, Google, Movember to name a few. People with lived experience and knowledge about mental health was more validated than ever. My career was talking off, but most importantly it just didn't feel like I was working.

I have since found that when we equate work, we love with "not really working," it propagates a belief that if we love it so much, we should do more of it — all the time. I loved my work, and even though it didn't seem like I was working, it was easier to fall victim to burnout. I sometimes went back to my home and would just put my head in my hands, unable to start work on anything. I was worried that if anyone walked through the door and saw me, they would get the wrong impression. But still, I congratulated myself on just how much stress I could deal with.

My symptoms, which could come at any time, were cold/hot sweats, 'jangling', extreme fatigue, and an inability to maintain my focus.

I just wanted to lie down and go to sleep. I felt myself failing and wanted to give up after rejection letter once again. I talked at home about 'when could I stop working' but never got an answer to say 'yes.' I don't know why I needed permission to stop but I did. So, I felt I had to continue. When I got home some nights, I immediately fell asleep on the sofa for an hour then got up to make dinner. Eventually, I was too tired to go to the gym. And at weekends I never missed an opportunity to 'catch up' on social media – on every journey I would sometimes have my phone on my knees to fill any 'potentially wasted time.

Burnout is a serious issue that can affect anyone. It is a state of emotional, physical, and mental exhaustion caused by excessive and prolonged stress. It was the reason that I would publish on social media sometimes, that I just couldn't do it anymore. I would take a break, feel great again and carry on with the fight.

Being diagnosed with ADHD, I was now able to share my experience as well. I was invited to become a research champion at the National Mental Health Centre and was learning more about neurodiversity. I was looking at the research of the condition which affects the development of the brain, especially in the frontal regions that are responsible for executive functions such as attention, working memory, and impulse control.

Adults with high levels of attention-deficit hyperactivity disorder (ADHD) symptoms are more likely to experience anxiety and depression than adults with high levels of autistic traits, according to new research led by psychologists at the University of Bath.

Until now, there has been a dearth of information on the effects of ADHD on poor mental health, with far more research focusing on the impact of autism on depression, anxiety and quality of life. As a result, people with ADHD have often struggled to access the clinical care they need to cope with their symptoms.

All my bad experiences in life were now used for the better, and it was around this time I came across the words "post-traumatic growth" by Dr Zoe Darwin, which give me the idea for this book.

I had written a book by this point, but with help with the publisher who helped me with my dyslexia, had the book Daddy Blues published. One of the most important efforts was writing about my experience with depression. Writing is one way I discover things, but a deep fear had blocked me from doing it for years. I can see now that the real reason I got stuck was that I had been trying to write about everything but depression. When I could finally take that on directly, writing came naturally.

I had found a deeply satisfying purpose in writing, as well as the energy and purpose to do what I wanted to do to make people understand that it can happen to anyone. That book was then turned into a film during covid, which was made with only £1,000, and it's still available on Amazon Prime. It was a wonderful experience again being producer of your own story.

After working as a wellbeing manager for a project that was supposed to last three months but turned into two years. I was given a free role and could develop the project in how we wanted to the patients to be treated. I saw that if they weren't getting the care, that my parents would want, I would highlight it in meeting and speak my own mind.

I was lucky, I was in a position that I could walk out. Sadly, that isn't the same for many people who want to speak out about patients care and treatment. On the positive, I was working with my friend and that meant there was no toxic environment apart from one lead nurse that was just jealous it took all my strength to report it to her manager for being bullied that it suddenly stopped. We have all been there – dealing with a boss, coworker, or acquaintance with an overinflated ego. They can be frustrating, difficult to work with and create unnecessary stress in the workplace which was happening to me.

After my experiences of working on the wards I could not imagine, what health professionals and even the cleaners went through during Covid. Whenever there was any virus on the ward, we would lose patients. One time we lost six patients on the four wards in a few days. One day you're talking with them and the next you see them disappear. The two years on the ward, there was times me and my friend needed someone to talk to about the experiences.

Again, I learned so much from patients with all different types of dementia, Parkinson's, and others who were struggling with their mental and physical health. I could have stayed there as the project was expanding, but I knew someone else could take my place and there was no one pushing for change for parents.

I decided to go full-time being self-employed as work was coming in thick and fast. I loved my job at the NHS supporting people on the wards and it was such a rewarding experience. The families were so grateful, but also frustrating that many patients should never had been on the ward for the length of time. It was all about the lack of care packages and mostly the lack of communication which was frustrating for me to take.

It was clear as day, that care workers were quitting to become Amazon warehouse pickers and for other better-paid jobs in a growing staffing crisis. This was costing the NHS more money, while patients just could not leave, rather than pay them better rates of pay.

"It's not how far you fall, but how high you bounce that counts." – Zig Ziglar

I was now full-time and touring around the country with other professionals and doing more conferences than ever. My face-to-face training was going well, and I was offered so much work, and then the day that everyone remembers happened.

The day the whole country came to a shut down. Withing days my bookings for the entire year went blank. I was super busy and then nothing, and we were told we could walk for a few hours per week locally. I had no support like employees of other companies, as I was normally part-time and that hit us.

The first weeks I struggled and then I started relaxing and having the time to do things that I had never done before, like photography and spending even more time with Michelle and my son. We started doing quizzes in the street away from each other and other simple things that I was enjoying even more than just spending money.

It was while in the garden I read the book Fathers for Justice, and in the back of the book were chapters about policy and making change. I had met Matt O'Conner at a conference and learned the importance of parental alienation. I had seen it from the fathers who had been unwell and separated from their children, and even with a mum who had postnatal depression and lost everything including her children.

With music in the background and the sun on my face, I needed to write something to give to policy changers with all the evidence backed up by professionals. After many months and with the help from Dad Pad and Hannah I wrote a report called "Fathers Reaching Out, Why Dads Matter."

The report aimed to provide a comprehensive and concise overview of the research findings, highlighting their relevance and potential impact on decision-making. By presenting this evidence-based information, it would empower individuals in a position to effect change with the necessary tools to understand the importance of effective communication and informed decision-making. The report served as a tangible resource that consolidated all the necessary information, enabling stakeholders to readily access and utilize it to drive positive outcomes.

After strict lockdown rules were lifted, we went to Westminster, and I was interviewed by The Guardian newspaper which they filmed me giving my member of parliament, Chris Elmore the report.

Among the campaigners was Dan who runs a Andy man's club, and we produced a podcast together called "How are you Dad". He, like James, had gone through postnatal depression. Julian made the film and the report happen and I will never forget that ever. My good friend Ashely Curry suffered with paternal OCD and is so knowledgeable in his field, and a great barber.

And Helen Birch, a wonderful lady who had so much support when she was going through postnatal depression, but not once was her partner asked how he felt, and he died by suicide. Helen has gone from strength to strength and is a true campaigner and has worked her way up with nothing.

115

The gang stood outside parliament and the National Institute of Care (NICE), which has nothing on fathers and no pathways of care when the biggest killer in men under forty-five is suicide. Together we were stronger, this is compounded by the guidance our health professionals receive regarding birth. The 88-page National Institute for Health and Care Excellence (Nice) birth pathway fails to mention the words "dad" or "partner". Because mums undergo such an overtly physical experience during childbirth, we professionals forget that dad is also undergoing a significant psychological and physiological change.

With business gone I started to work in the hospitals again. All I really wanted was someone to leave me alone and do what I am passion about full-time. If I had enough money to pay the bills and have some enjoyment with my family, I was happy. At this point I had overachieved in my life and never planned the way it had turned out.

On a personal level I had travelled to over forty countries, played for my country, done all the things I wanted to do in my life and had spent the most important time with family and friends that you never get back. The most important thing was that I was now walking the mountains healthy and was loving life again.

Lockdown give me time to reflect on everything, that I didn't need lists of things to do. I was even more happy without them, which give me less pressure in my life. I started to create an anti-bucket list. I never really celebrated my achievements and just went on to the next thing. It was now time to step back and reflect on everything that I had achieved.

When it came to my business, I knew that I had to start again, so I stopped moaning about it started doing something about it instead. It wasn't anyone's fault, and it was only down to me if I didn't change it. I started working online and was now reaching more people around the world than ever before.

The lockdown was hard for everyone, and dads were left out of scans, appointments and left out in car parks for days waiting for the birth of their child. This had an impact on their partners' mental health during pregnancy and that was not good for the mums and the babies.

Again, fathers were left out and there was more antenatal anxiety in fathers than I had ever witnessed due to more pressures than I had ever experienced. We did online support with a midwife for parents and spoke to over seven hundred parents. Everyone had their concerns and didn't have any visits from professionals or education unless they paid so much money privately. It wasn't fair that the working class was being treated like I had witnessed all my life.

As time went by during this part of history, my whole way of looking at things changed forever. I started to think of myself and reflect on everything I had done. It is often said that professional sports people often only really appreciate what they have done after their careers have ended as they are on to the next things as soon as they have won.

I had helped change policies that would save hundreds of lives each year with the long-term plan and had started my journey when not many people were talking about mental health. I had helped other people grow, and the ripple effect of my own work had now given the foundations for many other campaigners to follow.

It was also the year that the mother and baby unit reopened that I had started the campaign with over 14,000 names reopened in my country and had called it a disgrace before meeting the minister. It also showed that one person can be listened to by governments in the right way and may have taken seven years to open again that with other campaigners the fight was won.

I started to think of being awarded the Point of Light award for voluntary work and campaigning by the Prime Minister and later to be awarded the British Citizen Award for Healthcare at Westminster. It really for the first time made me stand tall and be proud of myself that I had achieved so much in my life, as I was now approaching fifty years of age. I didn't have to prove anything to anyone; after all, that was not the goal in the first place.

A lot of people promised to help or fund me in my objectives, but that never happened, and I just wanted to quit as I just couldn't afford to carry on self-funding the work. The support from Michelle to carry on and other people like Scott a dad who now works in the field helped me carry on further.

With Scott, I had someone who just got it, he was passionate and a father of seven who had so much experience after coming out of the army. No one knew the struggles of rejections and hours of pushing the campaign than Michelle, Jane, and Scott. I had to think back of my purpose when I started, and it was if I could help one dad it would be enough.

Everything was coming back together, then one morning while my mother-in-law was staying over, I found she had passed away on the sofa. I had gone downstairs to get ready for work and couldn't wake her up. She was always up before me.

I started to shout and scream for Michelle to get up and everything went into a daze. Running down to get the defibrillator from the youth club, I just couldn't believe what was going on as Jayne was fit and healthy, watching television with us the night before. I didn't think it was real and I expected her to wake up.

Phoning my sister-in-law, I had never heard the way she had reacted over the phone, and I phoned the ambulance. Watching my wife react in front of her mother who had always been there to support Michelle is anchored in my mind. It was clear that she had passed, but I carried on anyway.

I was already thinking about Michelle and how this was going to affect her mental health, and of course how my son was going to react to the news as we told him to stay upstairs and not to come down. It was just the most unreal horrible experience that we encountered as a family, as it was just out of the blue and unexpected.

One thing I was grateful for was I was the one who found her and that Ethan's friend, who knocked on the door each morning and walked upstairs to meet Ethan, was not there to see Jayne. There a teaching day and the school was closed, I could not imagine if his friend just come in through to the living room.

Jayne left a big hole in the family and died at such a young age, just a great-grandmother for the first time, and she was a lovely lady who we both had a wonderful relationship with even though we were the total opposite to each other. In the twenty-plus years we had three disagreements, and all of them were when Michelle was unwell. We probably would have reacted differently to them in ordinary circumstances, but with the

118

pressures we were both under at the time neither of us were thinking straight and we soon made up.

It showed us that again, life is so short and that we must make the best of it while we are visiting here and that some of the things, we tend to worry about are not always that important.

I knew that I had dealt with every trauma and processed everything up to this point and now I had to deal with this one. This of course made it easier for me as there was nothing else at the back of my mind. It was hard and of course is still hard now today that she has gone, but we tend to talk about the happy memories while she was here, and that death is part of the end journey that happens to us all.

That's something we see in this country and don't talk about the stages of grief enough, and that grief is not just about death, it's about everything including loss of your former self this of course can affect new parents as well.

As always in my work, I end up with a positive. When I deliver my talks it's like a shit sandwich. I tend to talk about the happy childhood I had with my family and friends and then the trauma that I experienced and how it changed my outlook of that trauma and how I used it to help other people.

I am glad that I have seen the real world and that it is not just sunshine's and roses, and I have witnessed things that my family and friends would never see in people's lives, and I am glad of that due to fact it has changed me from the days in Sales. I was working with asylum children who have no family around them. Their only goals when I am coaching them was to be safe, have a home, an education, and that's all they wanted.

I think we can learn from those children who have gone through war and torture, small aims are something we take for granted in this country. They are the humblest children I have been around, and they are so grateful to even be given a book. They may not speak English at the start, but some speak four different languages.

There were young people who had ADHD, I could relate to them and everything that had caused them harm. They had gone off the rails and were sometimes using drugs and alcohol to cope. I was hearing their stories and again it was like history repeating itself and now listens were being learned.

In the campaigning side, as I about to finish this book, I would get the message the I have been waiting for over thirteen years of fighting. It was that the father's mental health during the perinatal period will at last be on the agenda. Thanks to the team at future men, that have been pushing for change for parents for over fourteen years it is now happening.

To led on this agenda and have the opportunity to have my work now in writing to change everything I was content. It will always be on record, that I had made everyone aware of the people who could make it happen and had not acted. Also, for next people in power they will look back and see the people who have let society down. It has been a relief and even through the fight starts again, all that I can do is keep pushing forward without get obsessed by it anymore.

On top of that, international fathers' mental health day, which I founded was now growing each year. It has grown from an idea to have many organisations involved. To be told that I have saved thousands and thousands of relationships, lives and for better outcomes for the whole family by many people is something that will never be taken away from me. Dr Daniel Singley made it clear the importance of the day and joining force together.

To work and meet people, like Andrew Jenkins who had gone through a coma I feel blessed. Andrew who may have died suffering head injuries after a car accident, now become a friend who has inspired me to get back in the gym. He is an inspiration after talking about his own experiences has helped me get focused to keep training in the gym.

I'm fit, healthy and at present my own boss. That itself is now enough for me to keep going forward and will never retire, as I just love what I do now and avoid burnout daily. To be put it mildly, I'm just at peace with everything and everyone. It also just about whatever comes along, is now an even bigger bonus. I have my family, friends, and my surroundings, and helping people.

What more can one ask for really….

"Only those who dare to fail greatly can ever achieve greatly." – Robert F. Kennedy

I know my next chapter now in life, which is to work with young people who have struggled and to give them motivation to do what they want to do in their lives.

I want to help people who have been through hell and have come out the other side and, when professional help is in place, thrive. I also want to help adults with ADHD who have not come to terms with the diagnosis and tell them that if I can do it you can as well, and to help new parents with their mental health and push on with the campaign forever.

I have a great balance at last in my life. I can switch my passions each week and never get bored and frustrated as I had in the past, which had often made me want to quit. I want people to do even better than me, as I do with Ethan, knowing that I had played a small part in their journey.

I had spoken to many charities on social media and in online groups in Northern Ireland and could not believe that for all the trauma they had gone through, known as "The Troubles," there was not much support in place.

There were 237 deaths from suicide in Northern Ireland last year - 18 more than the number recorded in 2020. Also, it is the highest number of registered deaths from suicide since 2015 - 176 were men, 61 women.

The suicide rate for men and women has been on an upward trajectory since 2019, according to the Northern Ireland Statistics and Research Agency (Nisra).

There were 14.3 deaths from suicide per 100,000 people in Northern Ireland - slightly higher than the rate in other UK regions.

Out of the blue – About speaking from Derry, a lovely woman named Mandy emailed. After hearing about the work that Mandy's organisation was doing, I stated I would attend without even enquiring about the fee. Along with Mandy, I was going to meet Marie, another inspirational woman who founded Resilio, a charity that was helping a tonne of people.

I quickly got to know Marie, who was just as inspirational as Mandy and had shed even more tears for her community and changing things. Just by talking to Marie, the ideas were simply flying off me. I was thrilled to be requested to travel to Derry and do my two days of training since I knew that the people who would benefit from the programme were not concerned with money but rather with helping others grow.

It was one of the most memorable two days I have ever had, after my invitation to visit Derry. The group was passionate and just cared about what was best for Northern Ireland and a reduction in the suicide rate.

I met Martin and Des when I was there; they had sponsored two outstanding young men for the project and had assisted a great deal of other young people. When they speak well about Martin and Des, I get chills down my spine. Despite having gone through a lot, these young guys were keen to gain from the programme.

If only I could have contained the fervour and criticism that they were giving the group. Martin showed me around his charity in Derry and then took me off at the airport. As I was leaving, I felt a little down. I was enjoying the feeling of being surrounded by so many diverse people as I bounced off them.

You are now a member of our family, they would tell me, and it was the beginning of a connection. I felt a part of their cause, especially since they attracted press attention and wanted to raise awareness. I had never ever met passionate people during my training. I also, found a connection in Northern Ireland. People really spoke to you on the street, and the atmosphere was like the valleys.

The month that lay ahead of me, as I recall it now, was going to be more than what I ought to have considered an accomplishment. My mind was about to stop racing, and with it went the blood and sweat of working alone and the consent emails I was sending to members of Parliament. I was going to lead the discourse and put fathers and perinatal mental health on the Westminster APPG agenda.

One of the lesser-known institutions of Westminster is the All-Party Parliamentary Group (APPG). There is also an APPG for every country in the world, including many territories such as the Falkland Islands.

Smaller APPGs will typically be run by an MP who acts as an officer but the larger APPGs are usually run by an outside organisation, charity, think-tank, union etc. with a special interest in the subject matter of the APPG.

The purpose of an APPG is to raise awareness of the relevant issue, to provide a forum between MPs, Peers and external stakeholders. For example, the APPG for fathers that we support is a forum between MPs, Peers, academics and campaign groups who share evidence and support for proportional representation and wider democratic reform.

I had been fighting to get fathers and perinatal mental health on the agenda for thirteen years and was close many times, even at Westminster when we sat in the room and the very same day, they called a snap election. It was our luck at the time that the member of parliament didn't get in again.

It was Chris and Owen from Future men that changed that for me. They wanted to add to the agenda of fatherhood and include perinatal mental health. The charity had been pushing agendas on fathers for fourteen years at Westminster and they even did a survey.

The survey reveals that over half (52%) of men in the UK feel pressured by society's expectations of them, and that 40% suffer from anxiety as a result.

Future Men's YouGov poll reveals a crisis of masculinity as more than a third of young men feel unfairly treated and forgotten by society, with social media identified as a key source of negative behavioural role models.

- 37% of young men feels society still expects them to "be the breadwinner".
- 49% of UK adults believe that 'not being able to provide financially' would cause a man to feel emasculated.
- 51% of young men believe that society expects them to "man up" when faced with challenges.
- A third (34%) of men under 35 feel that struggling with mental health makes them less masculine.
- Over half (51%) felt that "crying in front of others" would make them feel 'less masculine'.
- 29% of UK men feel forgotten/left behind due to society's expectations of them.

123

The work that was being done was great breaking and the building blocks for a better future. We knew that it was clear that supporting all new parents has far better outcomes for the whole family and the development of the child. So many were on board and of course again it was trying to convince the people on power that it would save the economy money in the long term.

The date was set and was invited to lead on the research and evidence. It was an honour and so many people were invited on this agenda. I knew that there was a certain amount of pressure on me to demonstrate the importance of fathers and perinatal mental health.

It was the Human Rights Act that motivated and when the theme for 2023 World Mental Health Day was Mental Health and Human Rights it drilled the passion to greater lengths.

The Human Rights Act told me that you are worth as much as any human being. When I read the literature about the Human Rights Act, it confirmed to me that I have a right to develop my personality and my relationships, and to participate in my community. It confirmed to me that the rights that I regarded as so fundamental to people in other countries that I wanted to protect also applied to me. I realised that the compassion and care of this country is something that we need to apply to ourselves, as well as.

I think the Human Rights Act is that tool. It is there to remind those of us of who find ourselves in unacceptable situations that we are supported by our society and its laws.

It like when you are waiting for the bus and two come the same time, that I got a reply. There was a meeting online and about mental health and human rights, whether this was fate or the hard work paying off I don't know. But what I did know, that withing six days of each other, I had now achieved what I set out to do for many years.

It was about putting everything out there and it was up to the people with all the evidence to make that important decision. I could not do anymore and by not taking the action that was needed it was on their head. I felt that I had put it to bed, the years of trying to get this area of mental health on the agenda and now it was there for everyone to see.

Like, everything I have done it's about moving forward, and it was now time to join other people to fight for their human rights. I had also been so interested in stories of overcoming adversity which first started when Gerry Conlon one of the members of the Guildford four who stood out to the media and shouted that they were mistreated outside the old bailey. I still have that image in my mind and where I was that day seeing it on the news.

The Guildford Four and Maguire Seven were the collective names of two groups people, mostly Irish, who were wrongly convicted in English courts in 1975 and 1976 for the Guildford pub bombings of 5 October 1974, and the Woolwich pub bombing of 7 November 1974. All the convictions were eventually quashed after long campaigns for justice, and the cases, along with those of the Birmingham Six, shattered public confidence in the integrity of the English criminal justice system.

Then of course the Hillsborough disaster in 1989 and still remember to this day that it was the same day I missed a penalty in the semi-finals as captain. It is one of those days that is still as clear as if it was yesterday. Seeing it on the news, it brought it home for me, the number of times I had been to a football match and fall over when a goal had been scored.

The Hillsborough disaster was a fatal human crush at a football match at Hillsborough Stadium in Sheffield, South Yorkshire, England, on 15 April 1989. It occurred during an FA Cup semi-final between Liverpool and Nottingham Forest in the two standing-only central pens in the Leppings Lane stand allocated to Liverpool supporters. With 97 deaths and 766 injuries, it would be the highest death toll in British sporting history.

For over thirty years the families of victims of the Hillsborough tragedy have been fighting for justice. It was Anne Williams who was a campaigner for the victims of the Hillsborough including her son Kevin Williams, who died at Hillsborough at fifteen years of age that inspired me with her book and was the same age as me when it happened.

Every time, I felt like quitting and didn't see the light I would think of all the campaigners of Hillsborough and start reading Ann Williams book once again. As they had always mentioned, the truth will always come out in the end, and it certainly did with hard work and fight in them.

Campaigning to better our society is something that I feel strongly about and something that I will now continue to do for the rest of my life. I wanted to be part of something as a collective and not feel on times that feeling of being lonely as a campaigner and now that's happening.

Discovering your passion in life is a tremendous gift. Knowing what you're good at and how you can use it to live your life is a great feeling, and not something everyone figures out. But maybe you feel like there are two things you really want to pursue, and you're not sure which direction to take. Is it possible to tackle two passions at once. Can you do two things equally well, or do you have to decide? A lot of people might tell you that you need to pick one. So, I decided to bring them both together at the same time and just went for it.

ADHD and Perinatal Mental Health.

With other areas of mental health, I wanted to tackle; I had the confidence now to fight for more justice after already making so many changes. I wanted to show that ADHD had so many benefits and was invited to speak at my first conference only on the subject. I had delivered training on the subject and of course sharing my experience, but this was different once again.

I wanted to do what other people had not done and that made me reach out to Lisa who had worked with Parents for twenty years. We decided to put an article together and the response was overwhelming. Exactly like when no professionals didn't out their head above the parrot pit and dismissed that fathers could have postpartum psychosis and recruiting the dads who did for the research it was exciting.

We were looking at mothers first after speaking with so many diagnosed after having anxiety and depression during the perinatal period, I knew there was high risks and had spoken to these parents who would not sometimes speak with the researchers or professionals.

Becoming a parent requires routine, organisation, time management, inconsistent stimulation and sensory input, memory recall and prioritising. All these processes require us to call upon our executive function skills, which is something us ADHD folks find difficult. Thanks brain!

We already know that the rise and fall of oestrogen plays a huge role on female mood, emotions and cognitive function. It impacts during the menstruation cycle, menopause, while pregnant and especially after birth.

Aumatma Shah, N.D. fertility specialist and author of Fertility Secrets: What Your Doctor Didn't Tell You About Baby-Making explains the dramatic rise in oestrogen and progesterone, "These two steroidal hormones are key to creating dopamine and serotonin, two neurotransmitters in the brain that are important to feeling calm and happy" and why many of us can feel invincible during pregnant. However, what goes up must come down. "Unfortunately, immediately postpartum, oestrogen and progesterone will both plummet. Simultaneously, there will be a surge in prolactin and oxytocin".

A new baby may bring lack of sleep, poor nutrition and increased sensory sensitivity, which all heighten and increase ADHD symptoms. It's a one-way ticket to emotional and cognitive dysregulation, increased anxiety and depression, possible mood disorders and a steep decline in mental health and wellbeing. As stated by Sari Solden M.S., LMFT, psychotherapist and adult ADHD counsellor, "Managing the home is one of the most unfriendly lines of work that anyone with attention deficit disorder (ADHD OR ADD) could undertake....

The multiple-task coordination required to keep a household functioning smoothly bumps directly against the executive-function difficulties inherent in ADHD".

Lisa explained that her crash and burnout didn't happen straight away. Lisa had spent a lifetime becoming a master of masking, in front of family, friends and work colleagues. No one must know how useless and inadequate she felt. However, due to my studies and vocational career in Early Childhood and parenting, Lisa was also acutely aware that my mental health was deteriorating and the detrimental effect this could have one myself and her family.

Therefore, Lisa bravely shared her feelings and emotions with health professionals. After all, this is their job, they've had seen it all before, they knew what to do. With three years of weekly weeping sessions at baby clinic, going to my GP and finally asking for a mental health assessment came to nothing. Because my presentation did not score high enough on the Edinburgh Postnatal Depression Scale and Lisa displayed a strong attachment with her two beautiful and well cared for babies, (by now aged 3 and 1) Lisa received a letter in the post stating, Anxiety state unspecific.

Advice given was to rest more, phone a friend or make myself a nice cup of tea. As the guilt and shame mounted, Lisa told herself, to get a grip! Try harder. Work harder. Find the magic key to motherhood and all will be well.

Having a baby and becoming a parent is one of the biggest changes and challenges in any person's life. So, let's look at the job description "Personal assistant for at least one other person under the age of 18 years and possible other adults in the household. 24 hours a day, 7 days a week. Limited or disrupted sleep and mealtimes. Cleaning, laundry, and healthy eating meals must be provided daily at scheduled intervals. Excellent organisational, memory and time management skills, for yourself and others. Tutor, nurse, emotional. behavioural coach personal shopper, taxi driver and mediator when required. Possible part time position or retirement when your children leave home.

Due to historic societal expectations, this role is part of the female ideal. Desirable requirements, to maintain your appearance and home to presentable and attractive standard. Paid employment in an economic role to cover usual household bills and finances".

Kathleen Nadeau, Ph. D and co-author of ADD-Friendly Ways to Organized Your Life explains, "Women with ADHD, no matter how successful in other areas of life, struggle on the household front". They may question themselves as a parent, compare themselves to others and left feeling inadequate and unworthy.

In an attempt to combat this critical thinking and poor self-esteem, many adults (and young people) with ADHD will fall into destructive patterns of behaviour - rigid thinking, obsessive behaviours, and ruminating thoughts. Break down in relationships or substance dependent. Also, becoming perfectionists or workaholics to compensate for feeling that they don't measure up. This can lead to ADHD burnout; not attending to your own needs and self-care and becoming physically and mentally unwell can affect us during the perinatal period.

Lisa didn't place no judgement or blame for this dark and difficult time. Everyone Lisa encountered did their best with the resources and knowledge they had at that time, including herself. Thankfully, after my maternity leave, Lisa was able to access counselling and CBT through my employer, which led to a referral for an ADHD assessment. Taking off the mask and sharing how I felt was the most vulnerable and best thing I ever did.

It took just one knowledgeable and compassionate professional to notice the root cause of my perinatal anxiety and sporadic waves of depression. Lisa still looked back with shame and regret for the precious time wasted; feeling so lost, confused and alone, all because ADHD is misunderstood. Now Lisa has the knowledge and tools to avoid anxiety and depression creeping up on me again, by telling her story aims to help others too.

What can we do better:

• Parenting Group Facilitator and 1:1 Parenting Practitioner. Experience of working with neurodivergent children aged 0-18 years and their families.

• Attitudes and stereotypes - guilt, shame and self-esteem. Not just for kids, adults have it too!

• Differences and inclusion - why are we still getting it so wrong.

• Parenting and the effects on executive functioning – increase in demands, organisation and routines, which ADHD folks already find difficult. How lack of sleep or exercise, irregular mealtimes and hormones can make ADHD symptoms so much worse.

• Family Dynamics. Our own experiences of childhood and how we bring this to our own parenting. Triggers. Recognizing ourselves in our children. ADHD parents and how they manage their ADHD kids.

• ADHD burnout, overwhelm and managing emotions – impact on mental health. What support is available – Currently only on managing medications which not the right choice for everyone. No behavioural support or counselling recommendations for expectant or new mothers and fathers. More research and understanding on the role hormones play on ADHD women and young people.

• How well informed are the helping professionals – Lack of neurodiversity training and awareness. ADHD comorbidities when it's not understood and left untreated – anxiety, depression, increased sensory sensitivity, mood disorders, OCD, ODD ….

• What might help – Tackling stigmas and stereotypes. Raising awareness and early identification. Increase in behavioural and therapeutic support services. Reframing traits and thinking styles using a strength-based approach. Understanding yourself better. How you help you mind work with you instead of against you.

What might help:

• Acknowledge ADHD and how it impacts you, your family and other relationships.

• Talking to a professional who gets it; Trained and knowledgeable in understanding ADHD and differing presentation in men and women.

• You may not be the best personal assistant, but you can be a great project manager. Delegate tasks to other members of the family to seek professional support. You can't do it all alone.

• Problem solves as a family and work as a team.

• Respect your own feelings and how hard it can be. Notice when you are starting to feel frustrated, agitated or restless. Overwhelmed, fatigued and when everything just feels too much.

What and who can help before emotions bubble over. If an emotional tidal wave does take hold, how can you ride it out safely, without causing harm to yourself or others.

• Focus on the strengths, in yourself and others. Acknowledge that everyone is doing the best they can in that moment.

• Putting on your own oxygen mask first. Plan in advance how best to avoid burnout, becoming emotionally overwhelmed, drained or unwell. Prioritise your own needs and make self-care and downtime part of your daily life and routines.

• Create Golden Time every day. Even if it's just 15 to 20 minutes, stop on your path to enjoy the scenery. Regularly create space with no schedules, responsibilities or tasks to complete. Enjoy the freedom of just being in the moment. Alone and also as a family. Laugh, joke, play and have fun!!

• Know your own boundaries and when to say No!

• Look at and identify your individual values and beliefs. Follow your own path without comparing yourself to others. Find what works for you and live a life that makes you and your family feel good.

• Don't sweat the small stuff – choose your battles and only do what you can manage in that moment. Celebrate the small everyday achievements as well as the big ones!

Resilience

I wouldn't do the book any justice if I didn't talk about resilience. After all, it's what it says on the front cover. I feel that today's world needs to learn more about resilience than ever before. One important way to teach resilience is by modelling it. Teachers and other adults in the school environment can model resilience by talking openly about their own struggles and demonstrating how they cope with challenges.

Another way to build resilience is through experiential learning opportunities such as outdoor education programs, service-learning projects, and cultural immersion experiences. These experiences can help people develop a sense of responsibility, empathy, and adaptability.

One key factor in building resilience is the development of positive relationships with caring adults. Teachers can play a critical role in building these relationships with their students by showing interest in their lives and well-being and providing emotional support when necessary.

Ultimately, the goal of teaching resilience in any setting is to equip people with the skills and attitudes they need to navigate the challenges they will face in life. By learning how to bounce back from setbacks and difficulties, children and adults will be better prepared to handle whatever comes their way.

Resilience is the ability to bounce back from adversity, to recover quickly from setbacks and trauma, and to thrive in the face of significant challenges. Resilience is not an innate trait that some people have, and others don't; it is a set of skills and behaviours that can be learned and practiced.

According to Masten and Powell (2003), resilience involves three key components:

1. Exposure to significant adversity, such as poverty, violence, natural disasters, or illness
2. Positive adaptation or outcomes despite the adversity
3. Maintaining relatively stable functioning over time, even in the face of ongoing stressors

Building resilience involves developing the skills and resources needed to manage stress, cope with challenges, and maintain a positive outlook even in the face of adversity. Resilience can be fostered at the individual, family, community, and societal levels. Some of the key factors that contribute to resilience include:

- Strong support networks: Having people who care about you and provide emotional, social, and practical support can help you weather difficult times. This can include family, friends, mentors, colleagues, and community resources.

- Positive coping strategies: Developing healthy ways to manage stress, such as exercise, relaxation techniques, mindfulness, or seeking professional support, can help you bounce back from adversity and maintain your well-being.

- Optimism and hope: Maintaining a positive outlook and believing in your ability to overcome challenges is essential for resilience. This can involve reframing negative experiences, setting realistic goals, and seeking out opportunities for growth and learning.

- Self-efficacy: Believing in your ability to succeed and accomplish your goals is critical for resilience. Building skills, setting achievable goals, and working towards mastery can help you develop greater self-confidence and resilience.

- Flexibility and adaptability: Being willing to change course, try new things, and adapt to changing circumstances can help you cope with unexpected challenges and stay resilient over time.

Resilience is a complex and multifaceted concept that involves interactions among multiple levels of factors and systems. Building resilience involves developing the skills and resources needed to manage stress, cope with challenges, and maintain a positive outlook even in the face of adversity. Resilience theory provides a framework for understanding how individuals, families, communities, and societies can build resilience and recover from adversity, and can inform a range of interventions and strategies to promote resilience and well-being.

"What is the point of being alive if you don't at least try to do something remarkable?" – John Green

Chapter 8

Every day is a school day.

Over time, I have visioned myself and seen what I needed for my own confidence and how it would help me not just at work but in life in general. It was why I decided to become a coach and a leader through a coaching, mentoring, and leadership course. This has had a profound effect on everything, not just filling in the space in that section.

My relationship with school was a complicated one; it was never a place I felt safe or that I could call my own. Taking those first steps and returning to education after such a long break was hard. It was scary and daunting, to say the least, but it was the best decision that I could have ever made for myself.

It was only recently at my school mates 50th birthday party Strangy, we talked about the same teacher who had said that I wouldn't mount to anything and would find out that he had said the same things to him as well. That took me back, it was the first time we had talked about it after all these years.

I started the training to be an adult teacher with a headful of assumptions, mostly fuelled by the stigma that still seems to be attached to attending courses like these. I was torn between feeling proud of myself for making this big step and feeling like a failure for not having anything to start when others had done their GCSES and A-Levels.

Individuals with social intelligence can sense how other people feel, know intuitively what to say in social situations, and seem self-assured, even in a larger crowd. People used to think of me as having good "people skills," but what I know now is that I truly possess is social intelligence.

What I know about the theory of social intelligence it was first brought to the forefront by American psychologist Edward Thorndike in 1920. Edward Thorndike defined it as, "The ability to understand and manage men and women and boys and girls, to act wisely in human relations." No one is born socially intelligent. Instead, it involves a set of skills that an individual learns over time.

Effective Listening: When a person who possesses social intelligence doesn't listen merely to respond but truly pays attention to what a person is saying. The other folks in the conversation walk away feeling like they were understood and that they made a connection.

Conversational Skills: Have you ever seen someone "work the room?" They have conversational skills that enable them to carry on a discussion with practically anybody. They're tactful, appropriate, humorous and sincere in these conversations, and they remember details about people that allow the dialogue to be more meaningful.

Reputation Management: Socially intelligent people consider the impression that they make on other people. Considered one of the most complex elements of social intelligence, managing a reputation requires careful balance—a person must thoughtfully create an impression on another person while still being authentic.

Lack of Arguing: Someone with social intelligence understands that arguing or proving a point by making another person feel bad isn't the way to go. They don't outright reject another person's ideas, but rather listen to them with an open mind—even when it's not an idea that they personally agree with.

I was finding that I was automatically self-teaching myself and enjoying learning how to better myself in these situations. I am also aware that it can be a lot of effort and hard work for many people. When starting in sales I was paying more attention to the social world around me, as I knew that I could be taking to someone who could even be helpful in my own learning. It made me a better speaker or conversationalist. But of the roles was networking organizations, or speaking to people regular, which was helping develop communication skills.

Most importantly, I was becoming a Master of Studying Social situations and my own behaviour. Learning from not just my own social successes and failures, but other people I was enjoying listening to what they had done in their lives.

Its only when you reflect on everything with your family, life and work I have realised that our mind is like a magnet. We can experience what we give time and energy to. I now get rid of the rubbish and focus on the good stuff, and it attracts more great stuff in my life. The law of attraction is real, and this has been proved this over the generations.

I know there will be more traumatic events in the future; that is natural. Your brain is on overload with thoughts of grief, sadness, and loneliness.

Once more, Andrew Jenkins mentioned it in his own narrative. He told me that his counsellor had informed him that he was mourning the end of his life following the car accident that had left him unconscious and warned that he might not be able to walk normally. After these talks, Andrew helped me comprehend that, although sadness is frequently brought on by the death of a loved one, it's also possible that we are mourning for past lifetimes.

Grief and loss can affect the brain and body in many ways. They can cause changes in memory, behaviour, sleep, body function, and affect the immune system as well as the heart. They can lead to cognitive problems such as brain fog. We also have to remember that grief and loss affect people differently. Never judge a person unless you have walked in their shoes. You should never dismiss or look down on them.

Sometimes we tend to avoid doing the fun things because we are more anxious about what will happen. I have learned that feeling anxious, the first thing I tend to do is to take a deep breath and let a calm feeling into my mind.

I still have trouble controlling my emotions when someone springs something on me. I still have obsessive thoughts; I give every bit of energy to things that I enjoy, and one failure can change my mood. But that has become so much easier to control with practice.

The trauma I have witnessed and been through is far less than many people go through, but it has affected me – of course it has. I feel that I have gained so much resilience. I didn't want, and still don't want, anyone to feel sorry for me; it was never about that. It was about going forward all the time, helping people, making them feel better by knowing that they were not the only ones going through their darkness.

I want to use every single experience that has happened to me and my family to show that there is so much out there we can do to improve our lives and that we can grow after support.

I have reflected on my mental health and physical health. Eating healthily and drinking plenty of water are two of the most important things we can do to keep yourself growing, learning and to just feel happy. When you look after your body, you naturally feel calmer and have more energy to move forward.

I was a late-night eater. It never failed – every night in late evening, I got a craving for something. Sometimes it was a bar of chocolate and a packet of crisps, sometimes it was sweets that had plenty of sugar. Then, I heard from a friend one day that changed my eating habits. I heard that a lot of people mistake dehydration for hunger, So, the next time I felt that late-night craving for food, I drank a bottle of water instead. It worked! I wasn't "hungry" anymore.

I have now learned, taking time to relax is important for keeping healthy and happy. They say that stress is one of the biggest killers in the world. We must learn resilience, which is something again should be taught in our schools.

Life is shit at times, but at the same the time it can be amazing and that is what we must hold on too. We all can take responsibilities, that can make us happy and the people around us. Its hard work, but it can work for sure.

The only people I know who have no problems are living in your local cemetery, and that life can be great. Do what you love, whatever that may be for you and for no one else.

I have concluded, no matter how hard we try to prevent it, the simple fact is that sometimes, bad things. We lose things, we get sick, and we worry about things that has not happened. Trying to anticipate where things might not go the way we want them to go is something that I part of the human mind. For many of us, we worry all the time, abut things that never happen ever.

I have grown and I am still growing even today, and know that if you're going through trauma, with hard work you will find that light out of the darkness. I wouldn't say that I am grateful for the traumas, but they have given me the opportunity to gain empathy and understanding and has also given me the knowledge that we can all grow, through trauma.

I have learned myself when I experience a feeling it ok. I recognize and accept that feeling and express and let go of that feeling. It can work Our thoughts also create the quality of your experience, So I become aware of what I am thinking. When I choose to be positive my confidence grows. I am aware that when I am unwell, this can be of course harder for me and many people.

Cars, phones, and society have changed over the years, but not education and looking after people. I am obsessed by safeguarding people and when the environment I am in is not hitting that standard due to the rules to may come across as if I am not applying myself to conforming to customary, formal, or accepted practices, standards, and rules.

I may come across as unusual, unorthodox, and eccentric but if we all follow each other, nothing changes much. We need people who can look at things differently and by working together can improve and work things out for what is better for society.

We all have something to give. No one should ever feel that they are not worth anything just because they weren't educated to the highest standard. I am proud to be different and have travelled the long route to have a few successful careers. In the past, I have had the privilege of working with various charities and volunteer organizations, but I have always felt that there was more that I could be doing for me. After my online encounter with Geoff Thompson, a doorman in Coventry to now film director I realized that my next chapter must involve going deeper within myself. I want to use my creativity in other ways to help others and be involved more in the things that I enjoyed and was not shown to me in school.

Becoming comfortable in my own company would give me the time and freedom to truly explore my own passions without interference. It has a way to try new things, research topics that fascinate you, acquire knowledge, and even practice new methods of self-expression.

Art, street photography, acting at small plays on themes that are close to my heart and who knows maybe art projects myself around theatre in the future. Knowledge should be given away freely and not kept for our needs and something that I have upheld in my beliefs for many years. It also benefits my family, when I have this space on my own and do something for me.

"There is no growth in comfort" – Geoff Thompson

I believe that it's okay to be different, and if I am described as unconventional then that is fine. Maybe we should try to be unconventional sometimes in our beliefs.

What have you done today? If you carry on doing what you have done today, your future will be like your past. If you want a different tomorrow, you need to take steps to change what you do today.

Is there something you really want to do, but you're scared it won't work out? Perhaps you want to write a book or change career. Maybe you want to be a public speaker, or even be fit and healthy along the way. Whatever you want to do – just start.

Think what you can do today and be yourself, whatever your passions in life. And the last bit of advice be unconventional.

Do you have a purpose in life?

A dad should always remain a dad; someone to cadge lifts and money off, someone to turn to when things are bad, and someone to who can talk about anything. But they are now able to see me as a person as well as a dad. I no longer must pretend – too much – to be someone I'm not. Ethan knows my strengths and weaknesses almost as well as I know his and I love him always anyway.

Being a dad is what makes my life meaningful. Even when Ethan weas little, he never stopped making me proud. He's all grown now and we like kids when we are together and still gives me purpose to just be there for him.

My role as a husband in Michelles life is to be a supportive partner and stand by Michelle through thick and thin. That is also my purpose in my life and be around the people that bring joy into my life.

The answer to that question might be a key to your health and happiness, according to an ever-increasing body of research.

The concept of "purpose in life" is sometimes abbreviated PIL by researchers. "PIL" is not at all a bitter pill, despite the negative connotations of "pill." In fact, the more I read about the many benefits of "purpose," the more convinced I am of its importance to health and happiness as well as to a sense of your own unique identity.

One of my biggest interests was watching others develop and surpass me in their professional endeavours. Many may find that strange, but in my opinion, encouraging individuals to assist others again is related to the ripple effect. It served to remind me that I was only a little part of their path and that it was their own mission to better society, their family, and themselves.

After her own experience, a wonderful friend who had assisted me in leadership wanted to do more for the mental health of mothers. After our encounter, it was evident to me how talented and passionate Emma Jay was about supporting moms. In a matter of weeks, they invited her to speak with the Maternal Mental Health Association and presented her to all my contacts.

Emma's story was soon shared with the royal family charity, and that interaction inspired her to become a champion for maternal mental health alliance. The key to the popularity of that little film was the comments left by mothers who felt better after watching it; within a week, it had received over 350,000 views.

My family is important because it provides a sense of direction and meaning to the family members. It helps them to work together towards a common goal, which can be a source of motivation and inspiration. Family purpose can also help to strengthen the bonds between family members and create a sense of belonging. Having that in mind, If I didn't have my family and support, I would never be able to do the things that matter to me.

The lessons, I have learned about growth in over twenty-five years of sales and mental health is that:
• Create healthy boundaries and your self-esteem will grow.
• Training your mind to be positive is essential for your happiness and self-esteem.
• When you enjoy and find your passion, it will feel like you're not working.
• Healthy body and healthy mind are key to success.
• It is important to value every one of your successes, however small they might seem.

But what is "purpose in life," exactly? To put it simply, "purpose" can mean a feeling that the things you do in life are worthwhile. When you have a sense of purpose, you feel that you've made a deliberate choice to act in accordance with your values and goals. It can work the other way around, too. Your PIL can lead to further goal setting. Either way, your purpose gives you a sense of overseeing your own life.

Your purpose does not need to be grandiose; it only needs to be something meaningful to you (and, obviously, not anti-social).

Work. A hobby that you love. Devotion to someone you care about creative expression Travel.

A 2009 study of over 73,000 Japanese men and women found that those who had a strong connection to their sense of purpose (which they call ikigai) tended to live longer than those who didn't. Additionally, in his study of "Blue Zones" (communities in the world in which people are more likely to live past 100), Dan Buettner identified the factors that most centenarians share, one of them being a strong sense of purpose. In 2014, researchers used data that tracked adults over 14 years and found that "having a purpose in life appears to widely buffer against mortality risk across the adult years."

Make time for self-care and activities you enjoy.

Sometimes when we are trying to increase structure in our life, we may neglect to engage in enjoyable activities due to feeling like our time is too occupied by other routines or activities that need to get done.

It is important to ensure that you are intentionally scheduling time for activities you enjoy when implementing structure into your life. In other words, you need to set aside time for self-care. This can provide a sense of connectedness to others and improve your overall quality of life. Some examples of enjoyable activities include getting together with a friend, playing a sport, listening to music, gardening, or going for a nature walk.

Gratitude

Gratitude is a fantastic way to become more positive. It has numerous benefits for both mental and physical health, as well as relationships.

Start a gratitude journal where you record a minimum of three things that you're feeling grateful for every day. They can be anything from small, seemingly insignificant things to huge events. Even on bad days, you can probably find things to be grateful for. This reflection can help put things into perspective and give you a chance to remember things you often take for granted.

Positive affirmations can help you to overcome negative thoughts in a myriad of unwanted scenarios, and research indicates that even the worst situations can be made better for those who are used to performing these acts of positive thinking. Here are some examples of positive affirmations you can try:

• I am intelligent and capable
• I am strong
• Negative thoughts have no power over me
• I think positively in all situations
• I've got the strength to overcome adverse circumstances
• I react well to mistakes

Talk to a friend, family member, loved one, mental health professional, or anyone else you feel you can trust.

Use art as a form of expression: draw, write stories or poetry, make music, rant in a journal or personal video log, dance, sing, or make any art you like.

Express yourself through physical activity: lift weights, jog or run, punch a punching bag, dance, cycle, or do any other kind of exercise. If all else fails, talk to yourself, rant out loud about your issues.

Pent-up negativity can burst forth and overflow when you least want it to. That's why expressing that negativity, especially if it's very strong, can help you to overcome those thoughts and switch to positive thinking. Here are some ways that you can do this:

Making others happy is a great way to make yourself happier. It allows you to shift the focus from yourself and your negative thoughts, and the positivity that will spread from your compassion will be contagious (and it may even beget more kindness!).

I'm too Busy to do it.

Believing yourself to be busy may be an accurate reflection of your life. It may be a way of hiding from the act of making the first steps for success. UK adults spent nearly a third of their waking hours watching TV and online video content in 2020, according to a report from regulator Ofcom.

If you've ever had a similar thought, you may need to reframe the way you think about healthy living and your passion. Being "healthier" doesn't necessarily mean adding more to your already crammed calendar. Instead of further bloating your busy schedule, try integrating healthier habits into your established routines.

I am aware of the need to schedule some time to rest. While founders and entrepreneurs love to work, we also struggle to stop ourselves from overworking ourselves quite often. The result? We end up burned out and can't stay focused on a task — and that's if we can even get ourselves started on it in the first place. You need to take the time to reboot yourself once in a while.

Try volunteering.

Finding purpose involves more than just self-reflection. According to Bronk, it's also about trying out new things and seeing how those activities enable you to use your skills to make a meaningful difference in the world. Volunteering in a community organization focused on something of interest to you could provide you with some experience and do good at the same time.

Working with an organization serving others can put you in touch with people who share your passions and inspire you. In fact, it's easier to find and sustain purpose with others' support— and a do-gooder network can introduce you to opportunities and a community that shares your concern. Volunteering has the added benefit of improving our health and longevity, at least for some people.

Be Kind.

Never judge people. Who have little to nothing, as one day you may find yourself having nothing at all. Always respect one another no matter what, never look down on anyone. The quote explains everything in a few sentences.

The happiest people I know are always evaluating and improving themselves. The unhappy people are usually evaluating and judging others. Everything we judge in others is something within ourselves we don't want to face. No one likes feeling judged. Back off and let people live. We're all on some type of journey, all evolving and growing - Anonymous.

There is a widespread misconception that counselling is ineffective. This is untrue, though. Addressing mental health issues and enhancing general wellbeing can be accomplished with the help of counselling. It's a common misconception that counselling is just for people with severe mental problems. Anyone seeking personal improvement or experiencing emotional pain can benefit from counselling.

It's crucial to remember that counselling is a long-term solution that may not show effects right away. Furthermore, there are a variety of therapeutic modalities available; it could take some trial and error to determine which one is most effective for you.

If our fast brain assesses our surroundings and sees "danger"—whether the danger is real, like a seeing a poisonous snake in our path, or merely a disappointment or stressor, like being rejected by a potential suitor—it sets off an automatic fight, flight, or freeze response in us to help us survive. But, when the danger is not real and our slow brains neglect to calm us quickly, we can become overly anxious, impulsive, and reactive in ways that can harm our relationships and our physical and mental health.

There are other facets of mental health than mental disease. Talking about mental health in general might motivate us to regularly maintain our mental health. Whether we suffer from a serious mental health illness or only occasionally experience mental health issues, everyone can benefit from discussions that include advice or information on how to improve or take care of our mental health and well-being. Having a better quality of life and remaining generally healthy depend on maintaining good mental health. For some, this may entail seeking treatment for a mental health condition they already have. Others may need to take action to improve their general management of mental health through stress-reduction strategies like exercise or mindfulness and healthy lifestyle choices.

The quicker the help, the quicker the recovery
Mark Williams

Cognitive behavioural therapy (CBT) is a type of talking therapy that aims to help you manage problems by changing how you think and act.

Trauma-focused CBT uses a range of psychological techniques to help you come to terms with the traumatic event.

For example, your therapist may ask you to face your traumatic memories by describing aspects of your experience in detail.

During this process, your therapist helps you cope with any distress you feel while identifying any beliefs you have about the experience that may be unhelpful.

Your therapist can help you gain control of your fear and distress by reviewing with you any conclusions you have drawn about your experience (for example, feeling you're to blame for what happened, or fear that it may happen again).

You may also be encouraged to gradually restart any activities you have avoided since your experience, such as driving a car if you had an accident.

You'll usually have eight to twelve weekly sessions of trauma-focused CBT, although fewer may be needed. Sessions usually last for around sixty to ninety minutes.

Eye movement desensitisation and reprocessing (EMDR) is a psychological treatment that's been found to reduce the symptoms of PTSD. It involves recalling the traumatic incident in detail while making eye movements, usually by following the movement of your therapist's finger.

Other methods may include the therapist tapping their finger or playing sounds. It's not clear exactly how EMDR works, but it may help you change the negative way you think about a traumatic experience.

Psychodynamic psychotherapy involves talking more about how your past influences what happens in the present and the choices you make. It tends to last longer than CBT and counselling. Sessions are an hour long and can continue for a year or more.

There are different types of psychodynamic psychotherapy, but they all aim to help you understand more about yourself, improve your relationships, and get more out of life. Psychodynamic psychotherapy can be especially useful for people with long-term or recurring problems to find the cause of their difficulties.

There's some evidence that psychodynamic psychotherapy can help depression and some eating disorders. NHS psychodynamic psychotherapists normally work in a hospital or clinic, where you'll see them as an outpatient. Private psychodynamic psychotherapists often work from home.

Family therapy, a therapist (or pair of therapists) works with the whole family. The therapist explores their views and relationships to understand the problems the family is having. It helps family members communicate better with each other.

Sessions can last from forty-five minutes to an hour and a half, and usually take place several weeks apart. You may be offered family therapy if the whole family is in difficulty. This may be because one member of the family has a serious problem that's affecting the rest of the family. Family therapists deal with lots of different issues, including:

- Child and adolescent behavioural problems
- Mental health conditions, illness, and disability in the family
- Separation, divorce, and stepfamily life
- Domestic violence
- Drug addiction or alcohol addiction

Relationship counselling

Relationship counselling, or couples therapy, can help when a relationship is in crisis (after an affair, for example). Both partners talk in confidence to a counsellor or therapist to explore what has gone wrong in the relationship and how to change things for the better. It can help couples learn more about each other's needs and communicate better.

Ideally, both partners should attend the weekly hour-long sessions, but they can still help if just one person attends.

Group therapy

In group therapy, up to around twelve people meet, together with a therapist. It's a useful way for people who share a common problem to get support and advice from each other. It can help you realize you're not alone in your experiences, which is itself beneficial.

Some people prefer to be part of a group or find that it suits them better than individual therapy.

Interpersonal therapy

This is a talking treatment that helps people with depression to identify and address problems in their relationships with family, partners, and friends.

Behavioural activation is a talking therapy that encourages people to develop more positive behaviours, such as planning activities and doing constructive things that they would usually avoid doing.

Mindfulness-based therapies

Mindfulness-based therapies help you focus on your thoughts and feelings without becoming overwhelmed by them. They can be used to help treat depression, stress, anxiety, and addiction.

Mindfulness-based stress reduction (MBSR) incorporates techniques such as meditation, gentle yoga, and mind-body exercises to help people learn how to cope with stress.

Mindfulness-based cognitive therapy (MBCT) combines mindfulness techniques like meditation and breathing exercises with cognitive therapy. The National Institute for Health and Care Excellence (NICE) recommends MBCT to help people avoid repeated bouts of depression.

Directory of International Mental Health Helplines

Are you or someone you know in crisis? The following hotlines around the world can provide you with help. helpguide.org/find-help.htm

Chasing the Stigma (CTS)

Chasing the stigma has launched the Hub of Hope - a national mental health database, bringing help and support together in one place, with a focus on grassroots support. hubofhope.co.uk

ADHD Foundation

The ADHD Foundation is the UK's leading neurodiversity charity, offering a strength-based, lifespan service for the 1 in 5 of us who live with ADHD, Autism, Dyslexia, DCD, Dyscalculia, OCD, Tourette's Syndrome and more. adhdfoundation.org.uk

NHS Mental Health Helplines

Mental health helplines UK offer advice, support and information to people with mental health difficulties and their families and friends. Some helplines are open 24/7, while others have specific hours123. Some helplines can be contacted by phone, text, or email, while others are online only. For emergencies, call 999 or go to A&E. For urgent but not life-threatening situations, call 111 or use NHS 111 online.

Dyslexia

Diagnostic Assessments for Dyslexia are carried out by experienced specialist teachers and psychologists across the UK. bdadyslexia.org.uk/contact

Maternal Mental Health Alliance

The Maternal Mental Health Alliance (MMHA) is a UK-wide charity and network of over 120 organisations, dedicated to ensuring women and families affected by perinatal mental health. maternalmentalhealthalliance.org

Birth Trauma Association

The Birth Trauma Association (BTA) supports all women who have had a traumatic birth experience. It is estimated that, in the UK alone, this may result in 10,000 women a year. birthtraumaassociation.org.uk

PTSD UK

PTSD UK is the only charity in the UK dedicated to raising awareness of post-traumatic stress disorder – no matter the trauma that caused it. ptsduk.org

Anxiety UK

Anxiety UK is a national organisation; however we still have the same basic aims. Whether you have anxiety, stress, anxiety-based depression or a phobia that's affecting your daily life, we're here to help and are here for you. anxietyuk.org.uk

Projects

The Forgiveness Project collects and shares stories from both victims/survivors and perpetrators of crime and conflict who have rebuilt their lives following hurt and trauma. Founded in 2004 by journalist, Marina Cantacuzino, The Forgiveness Project provides resources and experiences to help people examine and overcome their own unresolved grievances. theforgivenessproject.com

The Good Grief Project is the brainchild of bereaved parents Jane Harris and Jimmy Edmonds whose son Josh died in a road accident in Vietnam in 2011. Jane is a psychotherapist and Jimmy is a filmmaker. Our mission is to support families grieving after the untimely death of a loved one, particularly the death of a child. And to promote an understanding of what it means to grieve in a society that often has difficulty talking openly about death, dying and bereavement. thegoodgriefproject.co.uk

On Side are passionate, properly funded youth provision. A unique partnership between young people and their community, local authorities and private business leadership, and a growing movement of supporters. Together, we believe that all young people need is a chance to discover what they've got and where it could take them. onsideyouthzones.org

Disclaimer: all the information provided is done with my best interest and the first point of contact must be your health professionals.

Acknowledgement

I wish to personally thank the following people for their contributions to my inspiration and knowledge and other help in creating this book:

Michelle and Ethan Williams for all your love and support. My entire family and friends who I can't thank you enough for your support in my life and my work. The people who sadly are not here with us anyone and the love you showed me. All my fellow campaigners and now lifelong friends Dr Jane Hanley, Dr Andy Mayers, Scott Mair and family, Andrew Jenkins, Emma Jay, Lisa Morna, Dean Hooper who are always on the end of the phone. And last all the people that I have supported and trusted in me in sharing their deepest troubles.

To my teachers who didn't believe in me, I was lucky that I believed in myself, but you have given me the push to prove you wrong. Your voices have been drowned by the people who got to know me and seen something in me. But thank you!

References

psychologytoday.com/us/basics/post-traumatic growth
nhs.uk/mental-health/conditions/depression-in-adults/treatment
verywellmind.com
nhs.uk/conditions/attention-deficit-hyperactivity-disorder-
adhd/symptoms
adhdfoundation.org.uk/resources
positivepsychology.com/what-is-resilience
fathers and perinatal mental health(Routledge)Hanley/Williams
Daddy Blues Williams
positivepsychology.com/motivation-theories-psychology
psychcentral.com/health/what-is-trauma
mayoclinic.org/diseases-conditions/post-traumatic-stress-
disorder/symptoms-causes